Letters
of My
Life

Letters

of My

Life

Mary O'Rourke

Gill Books

Gill Books
Hume Avenue
Park West
Dublin 12
www.gillbooks.ie

Gill Books is an imprint of M.H. Gill & Co.

978 07171 7223 8

Designed by Síofra Murphy
Structural editor: Alison Walsh
Copy-editor: Fiona Biggs
Proofreader: Esther Ní Dhonnacha
Printed by CPI Group (UK) Ltd, Croydon CR0 4YY

The lines quoted from three poems by Patrick Kavanagh is reprinted from *Collected Poems*, edited by Antoinette Quinn (Allen Lane, 2004), by kind permission of the Trustees of the Estate of the late Katherine B. Kavanagh, through the Jonathan Williams Literary Agency.

p. 16 © Matt McClain for the *Washington Post* via Getty Images; p. 28 © Design Pics Inc / Alamy Stock Photo; p. 50 courtesy of Newstalk / *The Pat Kenny Show*; p. 130 © *Irish Times*; p. 168 © INPHO / James Crombie; p. 192 © Bryan O'Brien / *Irish Times*; p. 220 © Tony Gavin / *Independent Newspapers*

This book is typeset in Palatino.

The paper used in this book comes from the wood pulp of managed forests. For every tree felled, at least one tree is planted, thereby renewing natural resources.

A CIP catalogue record for this book is available from the British Library.

5 4 3 2

Contents

To Feargal and Maeve, Aengus and Lisa,
and their six lively children, Jennifer,
Luke, Sarah, Sam, James and Scott

But most of all to my lovely Enda

To the Reader

Dear reader,

I wanted to call this book *As I Near 80*, not because I expect to receive congratulations on having got to this age, but because I had a sense of looking back over my life, assessing my family history, remembering the people I've met and all the things I find interesting in my life as I grow older. I am glad to say that I am not just looking backwards, which is a feature of old age, I suppose, but I am also living in the present, and I'm still interested and engaged with life, which comes as a relief to me.

As some of you will know, I wrote a memoir of my life in 2012, *Just Mary*, and I liked doing that very much. I have always loved writing, and indeed taught English many years ago, and it was a privilege to be able to look back on 40 years in politics. However, political life and everything that went with it consumed me for all of those years, and I worried that there might not be life beyond it, but I'm happy to say there is. That's why I decided to sit down and write to many of the people in my life, past and present, to thank them for everything they have done and meant to me. I have also enjoyed writing to interesting public figures and giving my opinions on them – I have never been short of opinions!

In 2001, I lost my dear husband, Enda, and for a while I couldn't envisage a life without him, but as you will see from my letter to my lovely gardener, David Henry, life flourished again. After a while, I had a renewed zest for life and, in my letter to the lovely actor Katherine Lynch, I talk about the great times we have before our monthly book club slot on Newstalk and about my love for poetry; I write to a French couple I glimpsed on the Bridge of Athlone one winter's morning, wishing them well as they begin their life together. I write to a lovely Athlone man, rugby player

Robbie Henshaw, and to Mo Mowlam, whom I was lucky enough to meet on a few occasions.

Perhaps this is a feature of getting older, but I have a greater desire to know more about my family, so I have written to my long-lost cousin Deirdre about her father, my Uncle Willie, who left for America so long ago, to my cousin Ronan about Uncle Roger, delving into the story of my family during the Civil War, and to my cousin Mairead about Uncle Joe, the German spy. Every family has a character like Joe; perhaps they call them 'black sheep', but this isn't fair at all: family is family, no matter what.

I have also written to the women whose friendship has sustained me over the years: Nuala Lally, my childhood friend, my sister-in-law Ann, my niece Gráinne and my old colleague, Margaret Walsh. Politics gives you little time for genuine friendship, but these women have been steadfast supporters and friends and I thank them for that. Of course, there is some politics in this book, as I write to my old friend Ray Mac Sharry, as well as to a new member of Fianna Fáil, but life now is about more than politics. I wasn't sure at all when I lost my seat in the general election of 2011 that this would be the case, but it is.

It gave me particular pleasure to be able to thank my old Maynooth professor, the late Bráthair Ó Súilleabháin, because without him, I would never have discovered the pleasure of teaching and seeing young women mature and grow, but my letter to my grandchildren means the most to me personally. Having grandchildren has been one of the greatest pleasures of my life; I wasn't at all prepared for how much Jennifer, Luke, Sarah, Sam, James and Scott have given me. They light up my life and brighten my day when they come to visit and I love hearing about all their adventures. They are life beginning anew, and it gives me great pleasure to see that.

So, dear reader, I hope you enjoy these moments from my life, the memories, happy and sad, and all of the people in it, family, friends and colleagues. How many of us get the chance to thank people publicly for all that they've done, or to look back at the milestones in our lives, or to understand the past? I am very lucky to have been able to do this, in my 80th year, and I thank you all for reading my thoughts.

Best wishes,

Maryor.

1. To the unknown French couple, kissing on the Bridge of Athlone

1

Dear ...

Well, I am not quite sure how to address you
both, because I never knew your names. I never
even met you; I simply glimpsed the two of you
on the bridge that winter's morning. It was at the
end of a week of fine, dry, sunny, cold weather
and I had been driving into Athlone town, when
I got stuck in a traffic jam on the bridge over the
magnificent River Shannon. Sitting there in my
car, I saw you both with your backpacks and
your lovely brown skin, the two of you looking
out over the bridge on to the river. My window
was rolled down, I remember, and as I passed, I

could hear you both talking excitedly in French to one another. You were holding a book between the two of you, probably a tourist guide, and you were both pointing out things on the river to each other. You paused for a moment, then turned to one another and you kissed – a lovely, deep kiss on the lips. How marvellous, I thought to myself, to see these two young people, just starting out in life, turning to each other in love and understanding, overcome by the history and the romance of standing on that bridge.

It was one of those moments in life that pass so quickly yet mean so much. I am sorry that I didn't stop to talk to you both, bad and all as my French is. Instead, the traffic moved on and the moment was lost – but I have never forgotten it or you and I sometimes wonder where you both are now and how you are faring in the great journey of life.

Seeing you both there, enjoying the magnificent river and sharing that moment together, reminded me of so many things: my town's proud history, of which you were both no doubt learning in your guidebook, the bonds between our two countries, but also the freedom of youth. George Bernard Shaw said that youth is wasted on the young, but

I don't agree. My glimpse of you both reminded me of how precious those days are.

For us Athlonians, the Thomas Rhodes Bridge, built in 1844 and named after its designer, is the one we cross every day to get to businesses or the post office on the Connacht side of the town. I have been crossing that bridge since childhood. The site of the old bridge of Athlone, immortalised in the famous poem, 'A Ballad of Athlone', which every schoolchild learns, lies downstream, and nowadays, the traffic whizzes across a brand new bridge on the way to Galway and beyond.

> Does any man dream that a Gael can fear,
> Of a thousand deeds let him learn but one!
> The Shannon swept onward, broad and clear,
> Between the Leaguers and worn Athlone.

As I'm sure the guidebook will have told you both, this poem, by Aubrey Thomas de Vere, refers to the action by six brave Irishmen during the siege of Athlone in 1691, when they managed to stop the approach of the Williamite forces by destroying the old bridge.

> Six warriors forth from their comrades broke,
> and flung them upon that bridge once more.

Again at the rocking planks they dashed
and four dropped dead and two remained.
The huge beams groaned, and the arch
    downcrashed;
Two stalwart swimmers the margin gained.

It is stirring stuff, I'm sure you'll both agree,
commemorating the brave Sergeant Custume,
who led a dozen men out to perform this heroic
deed. I have always thought that Custume was
in spirit with brave Horatius, dashing across the
Shannon as Horatius dashed across the Tiber a
thousand years earlier, immortalised in another
epic poem by Lord Macaulay, to fight off those
who would endanger the Roman republic.
Perhaps you might think me foolish comparing
the two, but the essence is the same: bravery in
the face of extreme danger, daring and bravery.

With weeping and with laughter
Still is the story told
How well Horatius kept the bridge,
In the brave days of old.

Now, I doubt that the two of you will be needing
to fight off an army of thousands – very few of
us these days will have to embark on battle, or
defend a whole town or city, but it's the everyday

battles that count, the small things that mean so much. We can't all be Winston Churchill, who learned the poem about Horatius off by heart to inspire his own battle in World War II, but we'll all have to face challenges. Life can take many turns, some good, some not so good, and each will need to be faced with courage. Living life to the full is the only option, and I hope that these poems, colourful as they are, will remind you both of that.

My favourite verse of all in 'A Ballad of Athlone' is this one:

> St Ruth in his stirrups stood up and cried,
> 'I have seen no deed like that in France!'
> With a toss of his head, Sarsfield replied,
> 'They had luck, the dogs! 'T was a merry chance!'

I wonder if the two of you knew about the French soldier, St Ruth, who commanded the second siege of Athlone along with Sarsfield, leading the Jacobite forces out against the Williamite ones?

Of course, Lord Macaulay's and de Vere's verses also remind me of the power of a mighty river, and I wonder if you were both struck by this as you stood there on the bridge, looking out into the fast-flowing river. The events of the winter of 2015–16 have reminded us of that power, as the river's surges left people bereft and stranded, their homes destroyed. Nature is a powerful force, and even though, over the years, clever engineers have found a way to tame our own Shannon, and to harness its power, more will need to be done in the years ahead, which reminds me of the world that belongs to you both, a world that is very different from the one I grew up in, when global warming and tidal surges and things like climate change were unheard of. Your world will present you both with very different challenges, and I wish you both the courage of Sarsfield and Horatius to meet them.

But seeing you both on the bridge also reminded me of my own personal history and the story of my love for my late husband Enda, and our meeting when I was just 18. It was at the end of my first year in college, and I had been working in my parents' hotel, the Hodson Bay, on the shores of Lough Ree, for the summer. I remember that he noticed me first. 'Who is that girl?' he said. But I noticed him, too – his dark hair and his smile – and soon, I was bumping into him in The Crescent Ballroom in Athlone, and from there, we progressed to 'proper' dates. Of course, I had dated before – harmless outings with young men from my classes in English lit in UCD, where I was a student – but somehow, I knew that Enda was the one. How, you might ask? Well, the two of you might well know as well as me! In any case, Enda and I certainly tested out our bond, splitting up when I was 19, before getting back together again. Then we both knew, without either of us having to say it, that we'd be together for the rest of our lives. Of course, in my day, once you'd made up your mind, that was pretty much it, and nowadays, people have more freedom in that respect, but it was clear to me when I saw you both that this was more than a fleeting thing. I wonder if you both have made your choice now, or are even still together – if you will both live happy, full lives as did Enda and I? I hope that you both do. Making my mind up about Enda was the best choice I ever made, and we led such a happy and fulfilling life together. Enda was my rock and my support in my political life but also personally, as well as being a wonderful father to our two sons. But of course, nothing is ever certain in life. All I know is that it's the making of the decision that counts. There's no such thing as a bad decision, I think – there are only decisions, and we make them as best we can at the time.

I hope that whatever decisions you both make in life, whether together or separately, will fulfil and inspire you both. And even if, in the years to come, you find that you didn't make the right choice, that you'll both understand that it was the making of it that counted.

I regret that I never spoke to you both, and that I didn't try out my pidgin French on you – you with your youth and spirit and me with my threescore years and 10. I somehow think that we'd have built a bridge between us – between your youth and energy and the so-called wisdom that comes with old age! I would have told you both of the history of my town, my home for so many years, and the home of my family, and you would have told me something of yours. Alas, it was not to be – we were truly ships that pass in the night. But I'll always remember the two of you, arms around each other on the bridge. I hope all goes well with you both, and I like to think that you will live out the rest of your lives in the spirit in which I saw you that morning.

Yours affectionately,

Maryor.

2. To Sheryl Sandberg,
Chief Operating Officer,
Facebook

1

Dear Sheryl,

We don't know each other, but I have been
following your career with great interest. I also
read your bestseller, *Lean In*, because it said
a lot that needed to be said about women in
leadership roles. I didn't like the title, though,
because I thought it was a bit weak. Why not
Jump In? I thought, or *Dig In*? I can think of a
lot of other verbs that might be stronger and
more active and more dynamic, because that's
what we need to be doing, Sheryl: encouraging
women to get stuck in, not stand at the sidelines.
In fact, I have been travelling around the country

recently, talking to women who are interested in politics, to encourage them and to stimulate them to take part in public life; my own party, Fianna Fáil, had not one single woman TD in the last Dáil Éireann. Thankfully, the party now has six, and I feel proud of the fact that my visits and talks might have helped to encourage those women along.

Of course, one reason that women may be reluctant to take part in political life is because they can see the long hours and the dedication that are needed and they rightly wonder how they might fit in with their other responsibilities. Of course, they don't like the snarling and the rows that they see nightly on TV either, and they feel they don't want to be a part of it. I also know that it is very hard to do this job without a supportive partner or without help. This is where I come to you, Sheryl. I know that you received a lot of criticism when the book was published. As COO of Facebook, you could employ nannies and housekeepers and gardeners to keep your household ticking over comfortably and your young family always provided for, which is obviously not the case for many women. You enjoyed a position of privilege, when many other women had to make do with part-time help, or with putting the children into crèches or asking family members to stand in. I think the comments were true, although, as is sometimes the case with social media, the tone was 'bitchy' and sometimes venomous.

I could understand a lot of what you were saying, because of my own experience in politics and balancing the needs of my family with my work, first in Athlone Town Council and later in Dáil Éireann. I couldn't have done either of these things without the support of my husband, Enda, who was always there to listen and to encourage. I was also lucky enough to have help. One day in 1976, when I was working full-time as a teacher in Summerhill College in Athlone, my doorbell rang. I opened it to see a small, neat woman on the doorstep, who announced herself as Pearl Samuels. 'You are going to be very busy now, being on the town council and teaching full time. I came to ask if you could be interested in taking me on as a part-time housekeeper.' I was delighted, and after discussing it with Enda, asked her to come every afternoon between 1.00 and 4.00, to be there for the children when they came home from school at 3.30 until I returned at 4.00. Pearl stayed with us for 18 years, long after my sons had left home; indeed, one of them had married by the time she retired! Pearl loved working for us, because it gave her a certain independence, which she relished.

Pearl was an essential part of our household, ensuring that clothes were ironed and the house was kept clean; for me, getting the evening meal was an easy matter, because the house was so tidy and ordered, thanks to Pearl. It also helped that Enda worked regular hours, so that when I became Minister for Education in 1987, we were able to work out a schedule that kept family life on track while I was in Dublin. Not that the process was without guilt or compromise, Sheryl, far from it. I can clearly remember that at the beginning of my career, I would make the two-hour journey home to Athlone and to Enda and the boys every night, after a long day in the Dáil. I suppose I wanted to feel that I wasn't neglecting them. Then Enda sat me down one night and said, 'Are you serious about your job? Do you want to continue in political life?'

'Yes, I am,' I replied.

'Well then, you can't be racing up and down the Dublin road to Athlone every night. I can be Mum and Dad during the week, and when

you come home on Thursday night, you can be
Mum again.'

What a modern man my husband was, and how
lucky I was to have him there, always encouraging
me and making every accommodation to me to
ensure that home life ran smoothly.

I understand that, like you, I was in a privileged
position. Yes, I had to balance my life carefully, but
I had the means to employ help and a supportive
husband, so my job was made so much easier. I
know that there are so many women for whom
this is not the case, particularly those women
who have to raise their families alone.

I was intrigued to read your Facebook post about
how much your position has now changed, due
to the sad death of your husband, Dave, in 2015.
You have become a single mother, Sheryl, and
you have come to understand how hard that
job is, attending parents' evenings and making
tough decisions about and for your two children,
without the advice and support of your husband.
Of course, my own two children are now grown,
but I understand just how difficult it can be.
When Enda died in 2001, I was bereft. I, too,
experienced the 'fog of grief' that you referred to

in a lovely speech to students at Berkeley College, California, the emptiness. I, too, returned to work a short while after Enda died, just as you did after Dave died, and, like you, I wondered what on earth everyone was talking about. How could they find something as trivial as a meeting important!? Yet, as you say, it is those little things that sustain us and that make it possible for us to understand that there is something else in life besides this overwhelming loss.

I had been in public life and very much able to do things on my own, but with the constant back-up and support and advice of Enda. Now, when I would come home fed up and exhausted from some political affray or other, there was no one to talk to, no one to share the burden. It was a very lonely time, as you said in your Facebook post:

> I did not understand how often I would look at my son's or daughter's crying face and not know how to stop the tears. How often situations would come up that Dave and I had never talked about and that I did not know how to handle on my own. What would Dave do if he were here? I never understood how often the world would remind my children

and me of what we don't have—from father-daughter dances to Parent Night at school.

You have come to understand that this is a situation many women face every single day, whether widowed or divorced or simply a single parent. (I know that many men are faced with this situation too, but they will forgive me if I focus on women, as this is a situation I understand.) And yet, as you also point out in your post, there is a hidden side to this situation, that so many people – in particular women – also face poverty as well as the emotional issues. You quote many statistics which are relevant to the US, including the fact that it is the only economy in the western world that does not provide paid maternity leave, but I have a few statistics, too. In Ireland, one in four families with children is a one-parent family and people in lone-parent families have the lowest disposable income out of all households in the state (www.onefamily.ie). According to the CSO, 42.5 per cent of lone parents work, compared with 69.3 per cent of heads of two-parent families. I'm not throwing these statistics out at the reader just for the sake of it; what I am saying is that for lone parents, particularly women, it is more difficult to raise a family and to work, as you have found yourself. Clearly, if we want to encourage more women to 'lean in', and to participate in the workforce, we have to make it easier for them to do so. The playing field is not a level one, as you yourself have discovered.

I think we also have to impress upon younger women the importance of having the skills to thrive in our modern society. It's not enough to be bright or determined, although that helps. And it's also not enough to rely on things like gender quotas or positive discrimination. I am strongly against that kind of thing, because I believe that women need to succeed on their own merits, not on their gender. Women need to be equipped with the skills to forge ahead in life, to be persistent and not to see setbacks as the end of the world. Setbacks are part of life, as we both realise; political life is full of setbacks: small triumphs and big failures, a sense of not being able to achieve everything you set out to achieve. If I were to have taken each setback personally, I would not have lasted long in politics!

I think women also need to develop their self-confidence and their self-belief. I can very well remember what it was like to be the only woman at the cabinet table, and to have to remind myself to speak up, to make sure my voice was heard, even though it might have been easier to stay silent. I can still remember the odd barbed remark from political commentators, such as the one I received when I lost my seat in the 2002 general election: 'Well, is it back to the knitting for you now, Mary?' I was livid, I recall, retorting that I had never knitted and had no intention of starting now. No man would ever be asked that question, Sheryl!

I have heard the expression 'glass ceiling' many times when referring to women's lack of progress in the workplace, and I have to say, I have never believed in it. Some might call me naive, but perhaps this is the reason why I succeeded in politics; because I didn't acknowledge it, nor did I want to fit the 'knitting' box that some might have wanted to put me in. I simply got on with the job in hand and didn't pay any heed to gender.

It used to be that men were considered to have the kind of skills – toughness and ruthlessness – required of a leader, while women were thought not to have them – empathy and emotional intelligence were no good in the boardroom. And yet that has now changed, Sheryl. I read a very interesting article in the *Irish Times* (27 February 2015) about women in business. Louise Phelan is Vice President of PayPal's global operations and this is what she has to say about the matter:

> It's not fair to categorise styles based on gender. For me, leadership is about empowering those around you and trusting their judgement. It's about investing in people and creating a culture of two-way engagement that rewards and values them.

She is absolutely right, Sheryl, as she is when she says, 'I never for one moment thought, "I'm not a man so I can't do that".' With role models like her, and marvellous examples of leadership among women today, including yourself, I hope that the next generation feels empowered and hopeful about the future.

Yours sincerely,

Maryor.

3. Eo Bráthair Ó Súilleabháin,
   NUI Maynooth

1

Dear Bráthair Ó Súilleabháin,

You died many years ago, but I have never
forgotten you and I have the chance now to write
to you to express my gratitude to you for being
my mentor at an important time in my life. I
often meet young people in the course of my day
and, indeed, I have teenage grandchildren, and
I'm always reminded how essential guidance is
to them; they are at a time of great change in their
lives and often a helpful word or piece of advice
can mean so much. Perhaps they might be a bit
lost or wondering where to go next in life, and
having someone older and more experienced,

who has 'seen it all', can set them on the right road. You were that person for me. But this letter is also one of thanks to my father, P. J. Lenihan, without whose intervention we would never have met.

Let me go back to one spring morning in 1966. I was a young mother at home with my elder son, Feargal, who was two at the time, when there was a knock at the door. I opened it to find my father standing there, a copy of the *Irish Times* under his elbow. He often stopped by when he was in town and I was delighted to see him.

He was in a state of great excitement and he exclaimed, 'Have you read the paper yet?'

'No,' I replied, 'I was going to push Feargal up in his buggy to the shops to get it later.' 'Well,' he said, opening the paper and pointing to a big ad, 'Look at this.'

The ad was on the front page of the newspaper, and it announced that from now on, Maynooth College, as it was known then, was no longer to be exclusively for the education of seminarians, but was to open up to lay students also. And one of the first qualifications they were offering was the HDip in Education for current or mature students.

I couldn't think what the ad had to do with me, but my father said, 'You should consider doing that.'

I was a bit taken aback. I had finished my BA degree in 1957, and had worked at the hotel before I got married, as well as doing the books for my brother Paddy's haulage business, but teaching had never been on my 'to-do list'. When I had finished my degree, I had flirted with the idea of doing law, which you could do at that time with a one-year LLB course added on to your primary degree. I suppose I was influenced here by my brother Brian, who had so successfully studied law, but in my heart of hearts, I had a yearning to do journalism. I had always loved the news and news stories, but in Ireland in 1957, there was no history at all of any college offering courses in journalism. And, more to the point, there were no female journalists that I knew of; journalism at the time was very much a man's world, and whilst I've never let that stop me, I couldn't see how I could go about learning to do that job. So, I tucked that desire to the back of my mind. Of course, life was to come full circle and I would return to journalism many years later, but that's for another letter.

So, my father was standing there, in the living room, newspaper in hand. 'You should consider going,' he insisted. 'Look, it says it's on Monday, Tuesday, Wednesday and Thursday for two hours a night.'

'But how on earth would I go?' I protested. 'Who would mind my lovely Feargal?'

'I have it all worked out,' he insisted. 'I'll pay for a woman to come in and mind Feargal while you go to college, and I'll put petrol in that old black jalopy you have,' he said, referring to the Wolesley car that Enda and I owned at the time. 'I think you should give it serious consideration.'

Now, Bráthair Ó Súilleabháin, as you know, times were very different then, and I dare say that my father was offering me this opportunity because he felt a bit guilty. When I had come home to Athlone with my newly minted BA 10 years earlier, my father had asked me if I would stay to help out at the hotel for a while; my sister Anne had moved to Galway, Brian was in Dublin and Paddy was in England, so there was only me, and, ever the dutiful daughter, I agreed. In fact, I was only too delighted, because I'd lit my eye at this stage on one Enda O'Rourke, whom I'd met the year before playing tennis at the Hodson Bay. We'd hit it off, and I was already madly in love with him. Why would I be haring off to Dublin, I reasoned? So, I stayed at home, working in the hotel and doing the books for Paddy. They both paid me and I was set fair in work and in love. I worked during the day and off I flew every night with Enda in his little black Ford Prefect. Halcyon days.

The point of my story, Bráthair Ó Súilleabháin, is that I needed my father's encouragement to start out on this new road. This might seem very old-fashioned to modern women, but in my day, your parents made a lot of decisions for you, and you did what you were told. I was fortunate in that my father was very forward thinking. I think he knew that I would need to have my mind enlarged and this was his way of doing it. I think he sensed that I was not going to be happy sitting at home with baby number one, and possibly, baby number two – the dutiful wife and dutiful mother living in suburban Athlone – but I needed his help to see it. I also needed Enda's support, which he gave willingly: when

I discussed the new idea with him, he was very enthusiastic about it and fully behind me.

This is where you come in, of course. I enrolled on the HDip course in Maynooth, which at the time was quite a distance away – this was long before the lovely motorway – and I put an ad in the local paper for others to share the car journey with me there and back. Before too long, there were four of us: Sister Christopher, a young nun in La Sainte Union in the Our Lady's Bower Convent, a man called Louis Walsh (not the boy band manager!), Beda Heavey, who wanted to add the HDip to her BComm, and yours truly. It was agreed that we'd each take turns to do the journey. It was just 55 miles, but on a narrow road through towns and villages that would become so familiar to us over the year: Moate, Horseleap, Kilbeggan, with the whiskey distillery, the lovely plantation town of Tyrellspass, then onto Rochfortbridge, Milltownpass, Kinnegad, Enfield and onto Maynooth.

Every single weeknight, except Fridays, off we'd go. I can still remember Feargal swinging on the gate in front of the house, back and forth, proclaiming, 'My mammy's goin' a gool.' He was very happy with Mary Flood, a lovely young woman who'd come to mind him while I went off on my great adventure. And because he was happy, I was happy too. This is one of the big lessons that I've learned from being a working mother, and one I hope will be useful to others: whatever you decide is best for yourself will be best for your child. Of course, we all struggle with feelings of guilt, asking ourselves if we are spreading ourselves too thinly, if we can really 'have it all', as they say nowadays. We can't, of course, but we can make our accommodations with whatever it is we've chosen.

So, on that first night, as 67 of us gathered in Maynooth, I felt such a sense of history and learning in this lovely old building, and in the mature grounds. I could imagine all the hundreds – thousands – who had gone before me, who had spent many years studying theology in this wonderful place. I felt such an affinity for Maynooth; much more than for my alma mater, UCD. In fact, many years later, I was delighted to receive an award from the university at a dinner called 'Maynooth Made Me', along with a few others who had benefited from an education there. Of course, Maynooth did make me, and in so many ways.

Anyway, there you were, Bráthair Ó Súilleabháin, on our very first night, a big, dark-haired, swarthy Kerryman, full of energy and vigour, ready to instil learning in a rum lot. And instil you did. You taught everything on the HDip course. If our lecture was psychology, or comparative education, or methodology, there you'd be at the top of the class, giving us the benefit of your learning. As Plutarch said, 'Education is the kindling of a flame, not the filling of a vessel,' and you would have been very progressive in this way, encouraging and supporting our learning, inspiring confidence in us that we could do it – we could teach and teach well. I can still remember your maxim: 'Never fear to overstretch a student's mind. They can take it. They are forever reaching for more information, and if it is above their reach at that time, it will always come back into their minds, so always remember that you can never overcrowd your students' minds.' What you meant by this, I think, was that we should always assume that our students were capable of more, and that lesson has stayed with me always.

When it came time to practise everything we'd learned in the classroom, you also supervised every single student's teaching practice. I can

still remember you coming down to Athlone
to watch me teach a class of lively teenagers in
St Peter's school. You stayed overnight in the
Prince of Wales Hotel and off you went with
Enda to the Green Olive, the local pub, for a few
pints! I was scared, of course, because I wanted
to impart knowledge, but also to keep control
of the class, which contained a few livewires.
I'd told them that you were coming in, and
most of them behaved. Somehow I managed to
teach them Latin for the allotted class, trying to
remember everything you'd taught me, and, at
the end, I learned that I'd passed. I'm not sure if
this was down to my teaching skills or abilities,
or the fact that I'd persevered and had come the
long distance every night. I can still remember
that every time you'd see the four of us – Louis,
Sister Christopher, Beda and myself – you would
joke, 'I'll have to pass the four of you for sheer
effort.'

Bráthair Ó Súilleabháin, I can honestly say that
you changed my life. Suddenly, I was in love
with teaching. Not fearful of it, not wary of it,
but delighting in it. During the five years that I
would spend in the classroom, I found that I had
an affinity with it, with the pupils and with the
subjects of English, History and Latin. I loved

my students. I loved the fact that they were growing in body and mind before my very eyes. I have always thought that that is wonderful – the transformation in the young person – and because I was still quite young myself, only 30 at this stage, I was still young enough to enjoy their company, to understand what they were reaching for and to be a part of it all. All of this I owe to you. I feel strongly that if you had not happened to be the person in charge of the HDip in Education at Maynooth, I would not have taken so readily to teaching.

And, thanks to you, I was able to use my skills as a teacher in my later career as a politician. If you have ever stood in a classroom of young girls and boys and talked with them, brought them with you on the road of learning, enjoyed their company and sometimes faced them down, you can deal with anything. Because of teaching, I was never afraid of speaking up. I had learned how to express myself clearly and strongly and this was all thanks to you. Being a teacher opened up my life and taught me such valuable lessons and gave me the skills to do my best in what would become my favourite job, that of Minister for Education. If I could leave the readers of this letter with one message it would be to always be willing to take the next step, and not to be content to rest on your laurels.

Writing this letter has brought me back to that day in 1966 and to the memory of my father, his face alight, newspaper under his arm. He always spoke quickly and forcefully in his Clare accent and he was full of excitement about the new opportunity he had presented to me. He was giving me the chance to continue my education, but also alerting me to what life could still have to offer me, in the academic sense, and later on, in a political sense. In this great new adventure of mine, my father was my first mentor and you, Bráthair Ó Súilleabháin, were my second. I hope that the readers of this letter will admire you as much as I did, but will also know that with a little bit of encouragement, they, too, can achieve anything.

Sincerely yours,

Maryor.

4. To Ann Lenihan,
my sister-in-law

1

Dear Ann,

I'm writing to you as you are 'family', but also because you are my closest woman friend. Now, I haven't amassed a huge circle of women friends in my life, probably because I haven't had time to do so. You see, friendship takes nurturing and nourishment, and during all of those years shuttling between Athlone and Dublin, between home and Leinster House, there simply wasn't 'space', as they say nowadays, for the kind of close friendship that many women share. Maybe you will think that this is a bit sad, but I like to think that you, more than many, will understand.

And, as I'm sure many other working women will agree, they are the choices we make in life. Politics has given me so much, such a rich and eventful life, and I'm grateful for that.

I'm also grateful for the gift of friendship that you have offered me over the years. Ann, I remember so well when my brother, Brian, fell in love with you and married you in August 1958. You were the belle of Athlone, and we were so pleased when Brian met you. There are also just six months between the two of us, so we had that in common too. Much is often made of the so-called rivalry between sisters-in-law, but I can honestly say that that has not been my experience with you.

Brian met you at the tennis club in Athlone when you were a student at Galway University and he was a qualified barrister. You were 19 and he was 24, and Athlone was full of rumours that Brian Lenihan was going out with Ann Devine, as you were such a catch. You came from such a lovely family and I was very impressed that your mother was a doctor, which was very advanced at the time, and your father was to become a chief superintendent. As the only girl in the family, you were doted on, of course.

I remember the beautiful bride you made and how much in love you were. I also remember, and this will amuse you, being in awe of you and Brian heading off to Positano in Italy on honeymoon. All those years ago, Positano was unheard of, an exotic place on the Amalfi coast, and we were in thrall to the stories you and Brian told us when you came back. I can still remember the two of you going for a walk together around Hodson Bay and out to Yew Point, on Lough Ree. It wasn't Positano, but it had that lovely unspoiled quality that our Irish countryside has. I thought it was the loveliest thing, seeing you and Brian hand in hand, starting out on your lives together: at that time, Brian was a barrister and an up-and-coming politician who would enter Dáil Éireann in 1961, and the future looked so bright for the two of you. I felt that it gave me so much to look forward to in my own life with Enda, and my own marriage just two years later, in 1960. We honeymooned on the Channel Islands, which, again, wasn't Positano, but I can clearly remember having that same sense of our lives beginning together and looking forward to that. I came across this lovely quote from Lao Tzu, which I think says everything. 'Being deeply loved by someone gives you strength, while loving someone deeply gives you courage.' I wonder if you think that's true?

Ann, I feel that our lives have gone in parallel. At times, our paths have diverged, but we have always come back together, because we have a shared history, and even though I hate the word 'bonding', we have strong bonds, you and I, being mothers, wives and friends.

Of course, you taught me to cook – I'll never forget that. I was brought up in a hotel, and as the food was put in front of me, I had never learned to cook. In fact, the first time I had to boil an egg, I did so in a kettle! So, you came down to me on a couple of Saturdays when I was a newlywed, and Enda was sent out for the afternoon while you gave me my lesson. I can still remember him returning on the first Saturday, to find that you and I had made chocolate éclairs – he was terribly disappointed altogether; he had been looking forward to steak and onions. But you were such a good cook and, to this day, I can still make terrific éclairs. The following Saturday, Enda came home to a big pile of meringues. He had visions of returning every Saturday to more cake and he wasn't a bit pleased. 'I'm not going out every Saturday and coming back to another Victoria sponge,' he grumbled.

In time, you and Brian would set up house on the Retreat Road, in a house that would become known colloquially – and jokingly – as The White House. Not long after, Enda and I would build our own home, in Arcadia, the home that I still live in nearly sixty years later. And then, in May 1959, you would welcome your first-born, Brian Junior, my nephew, and I can still remember calling in to see you, the joy on your face as you showed him off. Next came baby Mark, who would live just five short years. Mark with the tumbling auburn curls and the angelic smile and love for everyone, who so sadly died of leukaemia. I have always admired the courage with which you faced this loss and, indeed, all of the losses in your life, and you have had more than your fair share.

When I had my own baby, Feargal, in 1964, we bonded over that, I recall, and you taught me so much about being a mother, in the practical and the emotional sense, and of course, you were with me when I made the first step in adopting Aengus in 1968. I can still remember my first visit to the Adoption Society. It really sticks out in my mind, because you were with me. I had spoken to Enda about it. 'Why don't you take Ann along?' he'd suggested. 'I'll go to the next meeting.' How well he knew what I would need on that first visit.

Of course, you also understood, better than most, the ups and downs of political life. Supporting your husband Brian as you did in the many elections he contested and in his posts as minister, you provided the same backbone as my own Enda. I know I couldn't have achieved what I did in political life without Enda, and Brian couldn't have done so without you. I think it's marvellous to have had that shorthand, the two of us, that understanding of the business of politics and of the importance of public service. I also think that we both came to understand what it means to give someone our support and encouragement, the way all couples do.

I can also still remember the lovely holiday we had in Madeira, and how much we spoke there about Brian Junior, who had died just a few months before. I think it did us good to deal with our grief at Brian's death. Of course, you knew him as no one else did, as his mother, but I will always remember our shared time together in Leinster House, Brian and I, he in the Dáil and me in the Seanad. We'd meet often for coffee or lunch and there was nothing contrived about it; we just fell into an easy chat, even though his colleagues sometimes teased him about his lunches with 'Aunty Mary'! I so admired him and his courage and fortitude at carrying out his duties as Minister for Finance, as well as dealing with his illness.

I think I had a special place for Brian in my heart, because I remember him as a little boy, coming down to me on his bicycle to learn Latin, because he needed it for Belvedere College, where he was to go to school. We'd sit side by side at the kitchen table and pore over Longman's Grammar and then he'd go off to my mother, Grandma, on his bicycle for French lessons, and the two of them would sit out on two deckchairs and talk in French. He was as he became, Ann, earnest and bright.

I can still remember the last time I spoke to Brian, just a short while before he died. He complained that he felt tired all the time and that no sooner was he awake than he wanted to sleep again. I was trying to think of something useful to say and so I quoted from *Macbeth*, Act 2, Scene II:

Sleep that knits up the ravelled sleeve of care,
The death of each day's life, sore labour's
    bath,

Balm of hurt minds, great nature's second
course,
Chief nourisher in life's feast –

I can still recall that I recited the whole speech and, at the end, he said, 'Say that again, Mary,' so I did. And then he said, 'You were always a good teacher.' Maybe he found some comfort in these lines.

In old age, Ann, the two of us are still both going strong. We have both begun to experience the ailments that come with age – the aches and the pains, the illnesses, and yet we're able to talk about them, work out how to deal with them and, better, have a sense of humour about them. We are also able to keep our spirits alive and flourishing. We are united in our love of reading – we have shared books and thoughts about books. As we always say to one another, 'once you have a book, you are never lonely and you have a friend for life.'

Ann, I admire and love you so much and think fondly of you often. In my mind, you epitomise resilience, in spite of your losses and health setbacks. You are still the same, Ann, with your love of a good chat, gossip and the memories we share together. Yes, you are family, you are my sister-in-law, but you are much more than that; you are a friend. Thank you, Ann, for all the years of friendship we've shared.

Love forever,

Marjor.

5. To Katherine Lynch,
actress and comedian

Left to right: Mary O'Rourke, Brian Kennedy, Katherine Lynch,
Pat Kenny and Stephen Boylan (Eason).

Dear Katherine,

I am writing to you as a new friend, an expression which fills me with delight. How marvellous it is to make a new friend in my 80th year!

As you know, we met a year ago, when we were asked to review books on Pat Kenny's Newstalk show on the last Thursday of every month. We made an unlikely trio – yourself, myself and Brian Kennedy – but we hit it off from the outset. An actress, a singer and a politician – I am sure there is a joke about that, but from the very beginning, we made a great team. People nowadays call it 'bonding', a word that I do not like; let's just say that I felt an affinity with you and Brian.

It came as a bit of a surprise to me to be asked to do it. Even now, I am quite amazed at my audacity, that I so readily took up the challenge and that I went along to the first meeting to see how the whole thing would work. I am sure you were looking at me, wondering, 'What will we make of Mary O'Rourke?' and I was thinking, 'What will I make of Brian and Katherine?' But that's the great thing about life, Katherine; it's a bit of an adventure. And it also shows that you should seize the day, or *carpe diem*, as the old Horace epigram would have it.

Now, we have just celebrated our first anniversary on the show, and I look forward to our monthly meetings. We take our books home to read and to do our 'homework' (I always give it that term, because it really means that I am serious about it – not that all children are serious about their homework!), then we meet up 15 minutes before the show begins to chat: I've learned all about Brian and his family and his music, of course, and I've learned about your new play and the new man in your life, and you've learned about my life as a former politician and about my sheer delight in my six grandchildren. The talk flows so easily between the three of us. To my mind, our meetings and the show serve to remind me that friendship can happen at any time in life, and so can opportunities, if we are open to them.

However, I am also writing to you to talk to you about my love of poetry, because what the readers might not know is that you are the grand-niece of my favourite poet, Patrick Kavanagh. You often speak about him, and I have told you that I actually knew him, albeit in a peripheral way. When I was a student at UCD, in the days when it was on Earlsfort Terrace, a crowd of us would go to a pub at the bottom of Leeson Street for a pint or a coffee. Kavanagh was sometimes there, with a friend, or often by himself, and our cheery 'hello' would be greeted with a grunt – but a 'hello' none the less. I had always loved Kavanagh's poetry, so I was delighted to see the man himself. As I have told you, Patrick Kavanagh's poetry has accompanied me throughout my life, and I look back on my student days, seeing this slight man with a hat sitting in the corner of the pub, with great fondness.

If I was asked to sum up what I like most about his work, it is that he made the ordinary extraordinary; a dreeping hedge in a lane, bicycles going by 'in twos and threes– / There's a dance in Billy Brennan's barn tonight', a dance from which he, the poet, was excluded. All of these ordinary things he translated into beautiful words and beautiful lines of poetry, and he addressed emotions with such great simplicity:

> Every old man I see
> Reminds me of my father
> When he had fallen in love with death
> One time when sheaves were gathered.

I feel nourished, exhilarated and excited when I read his words. You may not know that before I went into politics, I taught English and history in Athlone for five years. The girls I taught were normally very receptive to poetry and I can still recall telling them, 'Say it out loud. Don't just be picking up a sanitised critique of the poem or the poet. Just continue to say the poetry out loud.' The reason for this, Katherine, is because I think that the more you say a poem out loud, the more sense it begins to make to you. I used to say, 'Don't worry if you can't understand the poem; if it seems esoteric or mystical or difficult to comprehend. Don't think about that; you don't have to make complete sense of it or to understand every word. If you find that you like the poem, only one thing is required,' I told them. That is, to read. This can best be expressed in the words of the great Olympic athlete Jesse Owens, giving advice to those who wanted to be great long jumpers: 'Sprint, then sprint, then, finally, sprint.' For the word 'sprint', we could substitute 'read', with equal definition. Read and read and the music, the underlying message of it, will convey itself to you without you even realising it.

This is the way poetry should be read, and you will so enjoy it if you follow these directions. I came across this wonderful quote from the writer Joseph O'Connor on the subject of understanding poetry. He was reviewing the anthology *Soundings*, which accompanied every student to English class during the 1970s and 1980s and was republished a couple of years ago. He said, 'Loving poetry is a marriage. There are good days and tough ones, rows and reunions, frustrations when you don't understand. Yes, you have to work at it, but how immense are the rewards. All of it is worth it for the joy of those moments when the world bursts into life like a fruit' (*Irish Independent*, October 2010). That is so true, Katherine.

But back to Patrick Kavanagh, because I have a little story about your great-uncle that I know will interest you. He lived on Baggot Street when he first came up to Dublin from Monaghan, and quite often he'd walk up Raglan Road, where a beautiful young medical student by the name of Hilda Moriarty lived. Kavanagh fell for her, really loved her, and that love is immortalised in the lines from the poem 'On Raglan Road', so memorably sung by Luke Kelly:

> On Raglan Road on an autumn day I met her first and knew
> That her dark hair would weave a snare that I might one day rue;

The story goes that Hilda Moriarty invited Kavanagh to her family home in Dingle, County Kerry, for Christmas, but he didn't fit in with them at all. It would seem that Hilda's father decided that Mr Kavanagh was not suitable for his lovely, academic daughter, and, like the good daughter she was, she broke off the romance. Kavanagh poured out all of his feelings into the lines of the poem, and I am always so moved when I hear Luke Kelly singing it, because it evokes memories of a time in my own life, Katherine, which I'll get to in a moment. Hilda Moriarty married a much more 'suitable' man in Donogh O'Malley, who would go on to be Minister for

Education. His greatest achievement would be to make secondary education free in Ireland.

I met Hilda O'Malley once, when she accompanied Donogh to Athlone to open a new primary school. She was waiting in the car for him and I stopped to chat to her. I have never seen a more beautiful couple together; they were like two film stars, dark and attractive and mysterious looking – Ireland didn't have such glamorous people in those days, Katherine, so you can imagine they both made their mark. How sad it is that Donogh O'Malley died very suddenly, with his innovative work only just begun. I can only imagine what he might have achieved had he lived longer.

Perhaps Hilda Moriarty's father was right to think that Patrick Kavanagh was not a good match for his daughter, and I suppose that if Kavanagh had never met her, we wouldn't have this beautiful poem today. But there is another twist to this story. Hilda O'Malley died in 1991, and on that day, Charlie Haughey, who was Taoiseach and leader of Fianna Fáil, came into the weekly parliamentary party meeting, stood behind the table and said, 'Yesterday, Hilda O'Malley died,' and then went on to quote 'On Raglan Road' in its entirety. He then told us the story that I have just told you, Katherine, and as he did, it dawned on me that he may also have been ensnared by her dark hair! It would not surprise me terribly, as she was a beautiful and gifted woman.

When Charlie had finished reciting the poem, you could have heard a pin drop in the room. I think we were all a bit surprised at this sudden show of emotion.

Later on that day, I found myself in the lift with Charlie and I plucked up the courage to say, 'That was a lovely poem.'

Now, Charlie was very much 'the boss', but I think he respected me, because he knew I had been a teacher. 'Thank you, Mary,' he smiled. 'I'm glad you enjoyed it. It went over the heads of three-quarters of them,' he said drily, referring to the members of the parliamentary party.

I have always read anything I can get my hands on about your great-uncle, and whenever I'm in need of a lift, I open my edition of *Soundings* and I read the lines about the 'stony grey soil of Monaghan', or the lines of 'Inniskeen Road: July Evening':

A road, a mile of kingdom, I am king
Of banks and stones and every blooming
thing.

But it is to 'On Raglan Road' that I always return, to the memory of my youth and my early days in college, and to the casual encounters with your great-uncle in the pub on Leeson Street, to the memory of that day in Dáil Éireann, but mostly to the beauty of the lines and the expression of unrequited love within them:

I gave her gifts of the mind, I gave her the
secret sign that's known
To the artists who have known the true gods
of sound and stone
And word and tint. I did not stint for I gave
her poems to say
With her own name there and her own dark
hair like clouds over fields of May.

Thank you, Katherine, for all the great chats we've had waiting for the show, and for reminding me of the importance poetry has in my life, how much it means to me and what comfort it brings to me every time I encounter it.

Best wishes,

Marty.

6. To my dear brother, Paddy

On his wedding day to his wife, Bríd.

Dear Paddy,

It seems a little strange to be writing to you, because you passed away in 2010, but it's not my intention to be grim or ghoulish at all. I want to share the story of your life with the readers, and to pay tribute to my favourite brother. It's a wonderful thing to be able to thank you in print for everything that you did for me when I was a child – how many of us get that chance? You took me under your wing when I was a little girl. Even though I was the baby of the Lenihan family and a bit of a nuisance, you looked after me with such patience and kindness.

Everyone should have a brother like you, dear Paddy.

The readers of this letter may not know that you were the second son to P. J. and Annie Lenihan. Brian was first, then you, then Anne and, finally, me. I was very much the baby, being a full seven years younger than Brian, six years younger than you and four years younger than Anne. I was also the only one of us born in Athlone, as our father had moved around a great deal for his work as a civil servant, before being asked by Seán Lemass to set up Gentex (General Textiles Limited), a textile-making factory in Athlone. It might be difficult for readers today to understand the energy and vitality that was present in the Seán Lemass era, developing industry in Ireland, employing so many of its people in home-grown businesses, like Gentex. It seems strange in our world of multinationals, Paddy! It might also seem quaint that Ireland once manufactured goods like tea towels and bedlinen, but we did – in the days before 'outsourcing' Ireland had a proud history of making things and exporting them all over the world. Sometimes, I am asked to do talks on Gentex or Athlone history and I often ask if anyone in the audience has Constellation sheets: at least three pairs of hands go up – Constellation bedlinen was made of 100 per cent cotton, long before the era of Egyptian cotton.

We lived above the shop, so to speak, on the Gentex site, in an old schoolhouse that had been converted into living quarters. Every day was punctuated by the sound of the factory hooters going off to denote the change in shifts – Gentex operated 24 hours a day, and at its height employed 1,000 people from Athlone and the surrounding area, as well as weavers from Belgium, which seemed very exotic at the time. Growing up for us meant rambling around the cotton sheds, and the huge looms, delighted if we were given a bar of chocolate as a treat by one of the workers. But, of course, our real playground was the banks of the River Shannon. We had a lovely rowing boat, which you and Brian had learned to row. Our parents had a great respect for the water and for its dangers and our father had taken us down to the cold waters of the river and had taught us, one by one, how to swim. I can still remember him teaching me, his strong arms around me as he urged me on; there was such safety in his care, I recall: when we are young, our parents are gods, of course, but I was very much in awe of our father, as you know.

We all became strong swimmers, thankfully. Our father had a strict rule about that, I remember. To set foot in our rowing boat, you had to be able to swim, and I can still remember my mother's warning: 'If you overturn, swim for the nearest shore.' In those days, there were no heated swimming pools, or spas or anything like that – just the wild river, with its currents and reeds. We loved our River Shannon! The poet Edmund Spenser was one of the first to mention 'The spacious Shenan spreading like a sea' in 1580 – I thought you might enjoy that, given your love of history. Of course, John F. Kennedy quoted from a poem, ''Tis, it is the Shannon's brightly glancing stream' when he left Ireland after his visit in 1963. He had actually been told it by Sinéad, Bean de Valera and he'd been so struck by it that he'd noted it down:

> 'Tis, it is the Shannon's brightly glancing stream,
> Brightly gleaming, silent in the morning beam,
> Oh, the sight entrancing,
> Thus returns from travels long,
> Years of exile, years of pain,
> To see old Shannon's face again,
> O'er the waters dancing.

Of course, he never did return to see Shannon's face again. Anyway, Paddy, I thought you might enjoy this poem, as you were always so bright and intelligent, and because it reminds me of the carefree days when we were growing up.

I remember that you and your pals, and Anne and Brian, of course, would all pile into the rowing boat and prepare to set off up the river, and Mam would insist that I go along, probably because she didn't want me under her feet. The others would complain, 'Please, Mammy, she'll only cry and then she'll be sucking her thumb and complaining about being tired and then she'll want to go home.' They'd refuse to take me in the boat – who in their right mind would want to take their baby sister along with their much more interesting pals? But, Paddy, you would always say, 'I'll take you, Mary,' and you'd take my small hand in your big one and we'd stride off to the boathouse at the back of the factory, and if any of your pals tried to tease me, to call me 'baby Mary', you'd always defend me. 'She's my sister and that's that.' None of your friends would question you, because you were big and strong for your age, and they didn't dare! I would feel protected by my big brother. That's really why I'm writing to you, Paddy, because you were my protector; I believe that everyone needs a big brother, or a protector, and you were mine.

How I missed you when you went off to Garbally College in Ballinasloe, as a boarder. Of course, I wasn't aware of it at the time, but you had been sent away because you were a bit 'wild', a bit wayward. Brian was the studious one, but you, just 15 months his junior, were more of a free spirit, as they say nowadays, and you were twice expelled from Garbally – and twice taken back! I could only pick up some of what my parents were talking about, because I wasn't meant to be listening, but as far as I could tell, the crimes involved going 'down the town' in Ballinasloe and smoking. You even went into a pub – my God! Anyway, you were taken back into Garbally each time, so I suppose my parents must have begged the school principal, and, in time, you got your Leaving Cert. We all know that you were the brightest of us all, with your love of history – I could ask you anything and you'd know the answer. And you were tall and well-built with fair hair – a handsome giant – and how I admired you.

I remember that it came as a terrible shock to me when you became ill with severe flu and had to spend a month in a nursing home in Portobello in Dublin. You had pleurisy as a result of the virus, and when I visited you in my school uniform, you were sitting up in bed, still the big, strong man that I remember, but somehow wasted. I was terribly worried that you might not recover, but you did. And once you did, you showed your unpredictable nature by getting on the boat to England. You must have thought it all up as you lay in bed for that long month, but you announced that the academic life and your degree in agriculture in UCD were not for you and off you went.

Well, Paddy, you were a man who lived his own life, but mother nearly passed out altogether when she heard that you'd got a job in the mines, of all things, in a town called Worksop in Nottinghamshire. She worried, of course, that your lungs would suffer, probably quite rightly, and mining was a dangerous job: it was the middle of the last century, when there was no health and safety of any kind, and here was her fine son, going down the mines with God knows what company.

I clearly remember that it was an anxious time, but our father used to travel to Manchester for the cotton market, and he went to the head office of the mining company and made contact with you; he came home full of stories and told us all that you were in great form and looked well. You'd made a go of this new life of yours, settling into life in Worksop with a lovely Irish landlady. Mother was mollified, even though I suspect that this might not have been the career she'd have wanted for you. Still, you were brave enough to strike out on your own, determined to succeed in your own way.

When I was writing this letter, I looked up information on Worksop, and it was such a busy place at that time: malting, brewing, chair-making and mining were just some of the things that happened in Worksop at that time, a bit like Athlone. I wonder if that's why you liked living there? Perhaps it reminded you of home. It's a little bit of history anyway, and now all gone.

I was a teenager at this stage and how I missed my champion, my own Sir Galahad. I took to writing long letters to you. I never cared if you didn't reply; I just felt glad that you were getting them and that I could give you the news of home: of Brian and his new girlfriend, Ann Devine, of my Leaving Cert results and my first year in college in UCD, of life at the Hodson Bay Hotel:

all of that, I poured into my letters. The odd time, you would write back, a grand, short note, but at least I would know that you'd got my letters and were thinking of me.

I also looked forward to your visits home on holidays; when I was 12, we moved out to the Hodson Bay Hotel and I wasn't a bit happy to be out 'in the country'. Even though it was only a few miles away, it seemed so far away from my friends in Athlone town. I cycled the four miles into town every day, I recall. As I became a teenager, I missed my girlfriends, the shops, going up town, meeting in the Italian ice cream parlour to talk endlessly and watch the world go by. Here again, you came to the rescue. I remember that you'd come home for your summer holidays and you announced to me one morning, 'Before I go back, I'll teach you how to drive.' We had to ask our father's permission, I recall, but he was only too delighted, as he could see the benefits of me being able to do errands for him in Athlone.

I was just 16 and couldn't get a licence until I was 17, so you taught me on the old Hodson Bay road, off the Roscommon Road, and you were so patient with me. I always think that learning to drive is a young person's skill: when you think of it, it is quite complicated: foot off clutch and other foot onto accelerator, off the accelerator and onto the brake and managing the gears … and in my case, in a big, heavy old Rover car. However, it never held any terrors for me because of your expert tuition. True to your word, when you went back to Worksop, Paddy, I could drive.

As I wasn't 17 yet, I was confined to driving up and down the road to the hotel, but every time I did, I thought about you and how well you'd taught me. I also thought about how lucky I was to have a big brother like you. But soon, my relationship with you was to change. I was in college at this point, and you came home for your summer holidays, and there was a lovely new head chef at the hotel, Brid O'Flaherty, from Carraroe, in Connemara. She was really stunning, with black hair and pale skin. You fell for her and she for you and, at the beginning, I was the only one privy to that wonderful secret. I remember meeting you one night as you were leaving her to the staff quarters in the hotel and you said, 'Don't say anything to Mam and Dad; you know the way they'll be going on.' So I held the secret tight to me, but I was full of knowing looks at Brid whenever we met in the kitchen! I was only delighted with myself to be part of this romance.

After a time, your secret was out, and you got engaged and then married and it seemed that all of Carraroe was at the wedding. You set forth with Brid on your married life, settling first in town and later in Hodson Bay and farming the land around the hotel, of which you made a great success. It seemed that farming was in your blood.

At that point in our relationship, I felt that you were 'gone' from me; not in the real sense, but that, in some way, you were no longer 'mine'. You now belonged to someone else. But, even though life had changed, we were still close and I used to love to visit you and Brid, and was delighted to be godmother to your first child, Pádraig. Now, many years later, Pádraig is Professor of History in NUI Galway and I am very much a proud aunt!

By this stage, I had become a twosome with Enda O'Rourke, and here's where you came into my life again. I remember that Enda and I had had a row and I was devastated by it. I confided in you and, quick as a lark, off you went to Enda's home and had a brotherly chat with him. I never did find out what you said to him, but it worked, and soon Enda and I were an item again. Of course, we shared a deep love, but I think that it is thanks to you that we went on to get married and to build a life together.

Our paths diverged again, Paddy, as I got on with my life, having Feargal and later, Aengus, and going back to college in Maynooth and so on; and you got on with yours, as Pádraig was followed by Gráinne, who, to this day, is a great friend, and then by Caoimhín. Sadly, Caoimhín was profoundly autistic, and, at the time, very little was known about autism, so your family faced many challenges; I can still remember you and Brid taking Caoimhín all the way to Boston to see a renowned pioneer in the field at the time, but while nowadays much can be done to nurture autistic children, in those days it was very different. But as we are a close family, Paddy, we all rallied around, and we tried to help. I can still remember taking Caoimhín for long drives to give Brid some respite and I was glad to be able to do it, and to offer you whatever support I could.

Caoimhín grew to be a beautiful, tall, strong, fair-haired man, very much as you had been as a young boy yourself. When he was 17, he went to the St John of God's facility in Oranmore, County Galway, where he received great care. Whenever

I pass the front gate of the facility, I bless myself, because poor Caoimhín died there. He was a very powerful swimmer and he loved to swim in the pool at the facility. It was as if the water gave him a peace and a tranquillity that he couldn't find in life. The pool became his refuge, which he found difficult to leave when pool time was over. On this morning in 1984, the staff came down to find that the heavy tarpaulins that covered the pool had been pulled back: it would ordinarily take two or three guys to do that. It would seem that Caoimhín had got up in the middle of the night and gone down to the pool, where he had swum and swum until he had a seizure and died. God knows what torment he was going through, and what relief the water must have given him all the same.

You were all utterly devastated; we all were; it is the hardest thing in life, for a parent to lose a child, but you and Bríd drew together and got through it; you continued to work the land and to see Pádraig, Gráinne and Fionbarr grow and flourish. And like so many of the Lenihan family, you were bitten by the political bug, joining the Fianna Fáil party and becoming a member of the National Executive. Here, your independent spirit came to the fore when you took Neil Blaney's side, and that of the extreme Republican movement, against Charlie Haughey. It's an old story now, but at the time, the divisions in the party were strong, and off you went to become an independent councillor. Our father and Brian were by this stage very established Fianna Fáil politicians, but I don't remember any of us falling out about it! I was in Westmeath County Council and Brian was a TD for Dublin West, but we were happy that you had found your own road in politics and that you made such a contribution to local life.

In old age, you faced the challenges of multiple sclerosis and Brid's Alzheimer's, but somehow you managed and I know how much you cared for her. You were a very loving husband and father, Paddy, just as you were a loving brother. Even though our paths diverged and then crossed at various stages in our lives, I knew that you would always be my rock and my support, just as you had been in my childhood. My big brother, Paddy Lenihan. God rest you always.

Your loving sister,

Maryor.

7. To my niece, Gráinne

Dear Gráinne,

I am writing to say 'thank you', or, as you would say in your lovely Connemara Irish, *'go raibh míle maith agat'*, for the long years of friendship you and I have shared. You are my niece, the daughter of my beloved brother Paddy, but we are also friends in our own right, as well as being aunt and niece. Thank God you never call me 'Aunty Mary!' In my memoir, *Just Mary*, I referred to the two of us as 'soul sisters', and that is true. We share the same, slightly sardonic view of events and of people – in a nice kind of way. We have a giggle about it – we share that giggledom of womanhood.

What is it they say about family – that they are there for each other because they have to be? But I like to think that we are friends because we choose to be, with the added bonus of a strong family bond. When I look at you, I think of Paddy: you have his fair hair and skin, as well as his intelligence. You know, of course, that your father was the most well-read of all of us Lenihans, and he immersed himself in history in particular. There was nothing he didn't know about history, from the Russian Civil War to the Native American reservations! Perhaps that's where you get your love of learning and teaching; you teach English and you are also a special needs teacher, which I think must demand a particular kindness and dedication.

I remember you so well as a child, growing up with your brothers, Pádraig, Caoimhín and Fionbarr. As the only girl with three brothers, you had such spirit, and your adventurous soul would take you far and wide. I recall your trip to Algeria in particular, I suppose because very few people went there at the time, which was the 1980s. I can still remember you having to get out of there quickly following the uprising, leaving all your money behind. I have always admired this quality in you. I'm not an adventurer myself in the same sense – I was to have other kinds of adventures! But I think those experiences must surely have shaped your character. Of course, we also have a career in common, in that you teach in a secondary school, just as I did for a few short years, and you know as well as I the stamina required to stand up in front of a classroom day after day, and the energy that's needed to impart learning to young people. It's a vocation, not just a job, and a job I know that you do well and with passion and concern for your pupils. I have always believed in the transforming power of education. I have always loved learning, as you know, from my days in Loreto in Bray, to UCD and then on to Maynooth, where I spent a happy year immersing myself in teacher training. I'm a great believer in education being for everyone. That has guided me in my political career and in my favourite job at the Department of Education.

Now, you are in the next generation, of course, but like me, you are a mother, and also like me, you have two sons, now in their teens. Feargal and Aengus are now grown with children of their own and your two are almost adults, so we have both been through periods of teenage rebellion. I hope that my experiences, and seeing my two boys grow into responsible parents, reassures you that all will be well. I well remember you telling me about your son, Rory, going to his first disco and worrying about that. I told you all about Aengus going through his teenage phase and the kind of mild rebellion that came with it, wanting to stay out and to be his own man – Aengus had the sense that life was 'elsewhere' and was impatient to get on with it, and of course, there were clashes, and worries about staying out at night, but somehow, we found a way through. Enda was in charge of discipline in our house, because I was away so much, and I have to admit that I often wondered if I was neglecting my family for my career. I suppose it is a dilemma that many working mothers face, including yourself, Gráinne. In my own time, I was something of a rarity, I suppose, and nowadays so many mothers work outside the home, but I consider myself lucky to have had so much support from Enda, just as you have from your husband, Jim, who is very hands-on.

Of course, we have also fought many an election campaign together and you have worked so hard for me, going out and canvassing for me. I remember particularly that last contest in February 2011, when you were with me in Kenagh in Longford the day I lost my seat. As you know, I had felt it in my bones that all wasn't going to go well. I'd been around the town and I'd sensed it. People were going to be meeting me in Dunnes Stores and in town, and they weren't going to be rude to me at the door, of course. It was unspoken, but I knew they weren't going to be voting for me. It meant so much to me that you were there, and I can still remember saying to you, 'Well, Gráinne, I've had a good innings.' And I believe that.

You now live in Ballybay, on the shores of Hodson Bay, which brings back such memories for me. I spent so much time in this area when I was young, working in my parents' hotel, the Hodson Bay, going to dances in Athlone, and, of course, that's where I met Enda, so visiting you at home always brings back memories, and although Enda is gone now, our friendship thrives. I always know that if I call, you'll respond and vice versa. During the recent school mid-term, you arrived at my door and took me off to the new café up the road for coffee and a good gossip, and I left feeling refreshed and buoyed up by all of the chat. It is all the more precious to me now, in old age, as you know. I must say, I don't feel like a little old lady, and I hope I don't act like one, but living alone as I do, companionship is all the more welcome.

Recently, Gráinne, you lost your dear mother, Brid, who passed away in spring 2016. I was glad to be with you during that time and to share your grief, but, above all, to share your friendship. I met so many of your mother's Flaherty relatives at the funeral, and understood what a blessing it is to have a wide circle of friends and family – Brid was one of 13! You have invested so much time and energy in friendship, and that is a great gift. I came across a quote recently that amused me: 'Friends are people who know you well, but who like you anyway.' How true that is, Gráinne. I can imagine that I might not be the easiest friend to know, but I also know that our deep friendship can be tapped into at any time, and that it will be enduring, because it is based on love and family history.

With love for ever,

Maryor.

8. To George Eaton,
chartered accountant,
Athlone

1

Dear George,

I am so glad to know that you are well again after having such a long and difficult illness. In my mind I call you the Miracle of Athlone every time I see you because there were many occasions when I doubted that you would make it to shore. But you more than made it and you are alive and well and full of your usual good cheer. I am glad to know that.

I am writing to you as you were the last but one company secretary of General Textiles Limited, or Gentex, as it is more commonly known. My father, back in 1936, was the first company secretary of Gentex, and I grew up above the shop, so I have a lot of memories. Gentex, as we both know, was the heart and soul of our town, and when it went it left a huge hole in the life of Athlone. The spirit of Gentex lives on, of course, in the social clubs that still exist today, and in many other ways.

Seán Lemass, as Minister for Industry and Commerce during the 1930s, was the instigator of Gentex. He was very forward-looking, as you know, and he saw Athlone as the ideal spot for establishing a brand new industry in textile manufacturing. The town still had lots of skills, thanks to Athlone Woollen Mills, which had employed many people before it had burned down in the 1920s, and, of course, it was on the Shannon.

Lemass had met my father at Dublin Castle when he was a civil servant there and had liked the cut of his jib, so, he asked if my father would take leave of absence to go to Athlone to help set up this factory. The family story goes that my father came home to my mother in Sutton one evening and said, 'Pack your traps, Annie, we're going to Athlone'. My mother had three children and was expecting me at the time, but she was happy enough, because I suppose she thought life in the country would be better for a young family. Of course, there was also the fact that she was a Sligo woman, and by going to Athlone, she was half-way to her own home county. My father was a Clare man, so it was a natural thing for them both to head west towards the Shannon.

The first directors of Gentex were a Mr Eustace Shott of Dublin and Léon-Louis Lagache of Brussels. Gentex had first been mooted by M. Lagache in 1934, as he had already established textile companies in Argentina and in the Belgian Congo. These first directors were joined some time before the end of 1938 by a Mr John J. Robinson (father of Nick Robinson, husband of Ireland's first woman president, Mrs Mary Robinson), and of course, my father had been appointed company secretary in 1937. By January 1938, a hundred looms were working away in Gentex, and by the end of that year, there would also be bleaching, dyeing and finishing processes. The Lenihan family was installed in the old Ranelagh Boys' school, above the shop floor, and a whole new life began for us.

All these years later, I look back on that time in Gentex as a golden one. We had such a marvellous childhood there: we roamed around all of the sheds, we knew everyone by name and they knew us. We always got a great welcome, a bar of chocolate if it was going and many a lesson in how to get on with people. I quickly learned that how people treated me depended on how I treated them, and this stood me in good stead for my later career in politics.

I think that so much of this came from my father. I remember that, no matter how late he had worked the night before, or how late he had socialised, my father would get up every morning and be on the factory floor for the 6 a.m. hooter. He'd be washed and shaved and he'd have a hankie in his pocket. 'Put your best foot forward and your best face forward,' he would always say, and it's an adage I've tried to follow, although I'm not setting myself up as a paragon!

I loved my mother, of course, but I think that I was truly on my father's wavelength. My mother was an intellectual, one of a small number of women in the 1920s who went to university, and she became a teacher, teaching in Loreto Convent in Bray, where I was sent as a boarder. She then became a tax inspector's wife, travelling all around the country, before landing in Athlone with three young children and one in her tummy (me). She was a mirror image, I often think, of what I would have been had I not gone on to Maynooth to do my HDip. My mother had a great outlet in bridge, thankfully, and I can still remember the twice-weekly card games she would hold, two tables set out for the players, and she belonged to three bridge clubs. Bridge was an outlet for my mother at a time when there were not very many. Later on, she played for Ireland at international level and we were so proud of her. She played top-level bridge well into her 80s.

Like many women of the time, she employed a housekeeper. We had Bridget Sharkey first, then Nora O'Sullivan, and they got me up, washed me, brought me to school – my mother got her breakfast in bed every morning. That didn't lesson my affection for her at all, but she wasn't as present for me as my father was, coming in and out of the factory every day. My father was a huge influence on me in so many ways.

The other story about Gentex, George, is that of the Flemish weavers. When you were researching the history of the factory, you came across a payroll from 1939, and of the 260 names on that payroll, 52 were Flemish. These weavers had been brought in from Flanders specially, because they had the skills and expertise that local people didn't at this time. A row of 20 houses was built to house the workers, called Talbot Avenue, which is still there. However, I can still remember that one of these Flemish weavers lived at the bottom of the orchard in front of our house, which had been part of the old school grounds. His name was Monsieur Trevier, George, and he must have been the foreman, because he had a better class of house – a stone and timber one – and he lived there with his wife. They had no children for a long time, but after many years, they had a baby, Yvonne, and there was huge surprise in the town about it. I was fascinated by the new arrival and Busybody Mary would go back and forth to the orchard every day to visit Yvonne. The family lived in the orchard until Gentex decided to go into spinning, as well as weaving, dyeing and bleaching. The only place to put the spinning section was the orchard and the lovely trees were all demolished.

When World War II ended, all but two of the Flemish weavers went home and that would seem to be the end of this exotic connection. However, many years later, I was attending a meeting of the Council of Ministers of Education in Brussels; there was a bank of translators up behind me as is normal in Brussels, and when I got up to go after my meeting, an usher came up to me and said that one of the interpreters wanted to have a word with me. And it was none other than Yvonne, the baby I had paid so much attention to all those years before. Someone had told her that the Irish minister was connected to the Lenihan family and Yvonne had put two and two together. Life is odd like that, George, and when I think of it, I'm always reminded of the poem by Robert Frost: 'Two roads diverged in a wood, and I— / I took the one less travelled by, / And that has made all the difference.' I'm not sure if it has made 'all the difference', but I feel that sense of the two paths along which Yvonne and I travelled.

During the war, some of the Rutus looms in Gentex were short of parts, and the only place where replacements could be found was in the US. I remember Gentex had hired an engineer from West Cork called Edward Sommerville, whom everyone called 'Chippy', because, at one time, he had been an engineer on a ship. My father and Chippy Sommerville decided they had to go to the US to get these parts. Remember, this was the time of the naval blockade, when Allied ships patrolled the seas to keep Germany from being able to import vital supplies for the war effort, and the only sensible way to travel was by one of the new flying boats, huge silver machines that took off and landed from Foynes on the Shannon estuary. I vividly remember going down with my mother and siblings to see Chippy and my father off from Foynes, and thinking, as the big machine went up into the sky, that I would never see my father again. In fact, he was gone for six long months and that seemed an age to me as a child.

Of course, he landed safely in America and he and Chippy visited various factory sites, finally locating everything they needed. My father would telephone the office to give regular updates on progress and someone would be sent upstairs in a flurry of excitement to let my mother know. She would go downstairs to talk to him, coming back with all of his news, and I would imagine him, all those thousands of miles away.

Then, the day came for the return visit to Foynes to collect my father and Chippy. I will always remember seeing him coming out of that enormous machine on the river and getting into a small rowing boat to reach land. As you can imagine, we were thrilled to see him again and that he'd returned safely. I can still picture the beautiful brooch he brought me back as a present, a figure of the famous ice skater and film star of the day Sonja Henie. For years and years, I kept this brooch and thought fondly of it, but, sadly, it got lost. Even though I don't have it any more, I still remember that time so vividly.

My father and Chippy carried the machine parts sewn into the lining of their coats, because they weren't supposed to bring anything back from overseas, and they returned in triumph to Gentex. With a lot of mechanical help from Chippy, the looms could go at full speed again, and, more importantly, jobs could be saved. This is a marvellous World War II memory to have, don't you think?

Great years of growth and sales went by during the period my father ran Gentex, as you know, and I can still recall the opening of the spinning mill in 1946. Seán Lemass himself came down to open it and I presented flowers to Mrs Lemass. The company just seemed to go from strength to strength at this time; at one stage, there were three factories in the town, employing over nine hundred people – imagine what an enormous commercial effect this had on the town of Athlone. The workforce was about 80 per cent men and 20 per cent women, and so many families were guaranteed a livelihood at a time when the economy was not good in Ireland. In its heyday, Gentex operated a 24-hour shift: every eight hours, the factory hooter went. One batch of workers would finish and the next would come streaming in the factory gates. I can still see that great river of workers ebbing and flowing.

This was a time, George, when employers felt a great sense of social responsibility to their workers and tried to foster a sense of cohesion in the workplace. My father was very much a part of this movement, which echoed the influence of Catholic social teaching of the time. There was an annual factory feast day at Gentex every year, and reports from all the social and sporting clubs would be presented – and there were many! There was soccer, hurling, football, boxing, camogie, swimming, tennis and badminton. They had Irish language classes, a debating society, outings and a brass band. There was a small oratory in the building, and a resident nurse, as well as a visiting doctor. It is interesting to reflect, George, on how workers were so fully looked after by their employers at this time; I suppose modern-day equivalents would be the Googles and Facebooks of this world, although that is for a minority; in most cases, the bond between employer and employee is much looser nowadays. Many of the clubs and societies still exist in Athlone, including Gentex FC.

I am not exaggerating when I say that all of this was due to the forward-looking, outgoing, curious spirit of my father, Patrick Joseph Lenihan. He was into everything, including setting up the All-Ireland Drama Festival, with Brendan O'Brien and Alfie Faulkner, whose first home was Sportex Limited, opened by Sean Lemass in 1952. The All-Ireland Drama Festival is still going strong, but, sadly, Gentex is no more.

My father retired in 1957, and we moved to live in the Hodson Bay Hotel. The company limped on in various guises, but the heyday of General Textiles was over. The introduction of synthetic materials like nylon spelled the end for cotton at that time, and Europe beckoned with increasing competition. The writing was on the wall. As it wound down, it was, of course, a huge loss to the commercial life of Athlone. I recently came across a documentary that RTÉ made about Gentex in 1970, when 300 people were being made redundant, and it makes for sad viewing, to see the men gathering outside the employment exchange, wondering if and when they might work again. But it gave me such pride to hear my father described as a 'benevolent employer, who would never see a man short of a job'. That is certainly true, George.

There are so many stories about Gentex, all the growth and development and technical achievements, but for me, the stories are personal ones, of my mother and father settling into Athlone, of the rearing of all of us in Gentex, of the wonderful childhood we had there and how it has, I suppose, influenced me all throughout my life. So many threads of life coming together in one place. The whole campus of what was once Gentex is now a thriving industrial centre, with a host of smaller businesses all doing well and all in new areas of manufacturing. It would give my father such pleasure to know that even though Gentex is gone, its spirit lives on.

So I come back to you, George. Thank you for that wonderful article you wrote in the

Old Athlone Journal about Gentex, which has formed the backbone of this letter. Of course, many of my memories of that time are personal ones – of my father, of Chippy, of the Flemish weavers at the bottom of the garden, of the flying boats … it is the story of Gentex, and the story of Athlone, but it is my own story as well.

With best wishes,

[signature]

9. To the Athlone Fianna Fáil Women's Group

Marcia Fletcher, Mary Lally, Marie Jackson (RIP), Dolores Walsh,
Freda Galvin, Nancy Gavin, Mary Galvin (RIP), Laura Lynam
and Eileen Seery

1

Dear women friends,

I'm writing to you all to thank you for your support at a time of crisis in my life, but first, let me just explain to the readers how we came to be. It was an initiative of Charlie Haughey's to set up informal groupings of women under the Fianna Fáil umbrella. His idea was to improve the representation of women in the organisation and, as with many of Charlie's ideas, it was an inspired one. Charlie was ahead of his time in many respects, and perhaps he is not given enough credit for that.

Our group was a great one, full of hope and energy, as you can see from the photograph of us all in 1987. There were ten of us, including myself: Marcia Fletcher, Mary Lally, Dolores Walsh, Freda Galvin, Nancy Gavin, Laura Lynham, Eileen Seery, Maria Jackson, who passed away far too young, and Mary Galvin, to my right in the photo, who died only recently. I remember with particular fondness your energies in campaigning for me during that election of 1982, our first together as a team. You worked so hard for me, day and night, in the foulest of November weather, determined that I would get elected. We knew nothing of gender quotas, glass ceilings or the parlance of modern-day feminism, we just got on with the business in hand. Perhaps this might make me sound as if I disapprove of modern-day feminism. That's not the case at all: in those days, we just didn't discuss it in those terms – we simply lived it. But there is a point to my discussion about feminism – read on!

As you all know, I had almost five very happy and productive years at the Department of Education. I felt that I had found my niche and was thriving, but, as we all know, life isn't straightforward, and Charles Haughey made me Minister for Health in late 1991. I didn't want to go, of course, but perhaps Charlie thought

I would bring new skills to the department, so go I did. And I put all my energy into my new brief, staying up long into the night to master the complex issues at the department.

Now, I had been only three short months into my new job as Minister for Health, when Albert Reynolds became leader of Fianna Fáil and Taoiseach in 1992. As was his right, he replaced 14 serving ministers with new ones – and I was out of a job. Now, I wasn't very dignified, ladies, about the whole thing; in fact, I sobbed and railed against the injustice of it all, and even though Albert made me Minister for Labour Affairs, I wasn't satisfied. I saw it as a demotion.

Of course, disappointment is part of life, and I knew that I needed time to absorb what I saw as a bitter blow at home with Enda and the boys. So, off I went to Athlone on Friday after work to lick my wounds. In the car, I received a phone call on the mobile – a brand-new device at the time – that I would be met at Horseleap, some 30 miles from Athlone, by a delegation of Fianna Fáil women.

I can't tell you what this meant to me. I was moved and humbled and I can remember vividly wiping a tear from my eye as we sped along the road towards home. We pulled in at Horseleap, and there was the Athlone Women's Group in all its glory, waiting to greet me and to accompany me for the final few miles to the Prince of Wales Hotel for our meeting. It was certainly an emotional homecoming, and it reminded me yet again – as if I needed reminding – of the true spirit of feminism: women working for and with each other, nurturing and supporting each other in good times and bad.

Of course, I have a permanent reminder of that moment in the lovely magnolia tree, which you gave me as a gift. And this I know will amuse you: Enda decided to plant it outside my kitchen window. 'Well, because you would be at the sink quite a bit, doing the washing up, you'll be able to see the tree as you work.' I chose to see this in the spirit in which it was intended, as a gesture of consideration! That magnolia tree is still there today, almost 25 years later, a reminder of so many things; of Enda, who passed away 15 years ago, of my own journey to learning to live without him, and of the importance of that network of women, who offer support like no one else. That is the true spirit of feminism, I feel, and one that was exemplified by the Athlone Women's Group.

To the Athlone Fianna Fáil Women's Group

As time passed, you got on with your own lives and the group was no more, but I would bump into one or other of you in the supermarket from time to time, and it would always remind me of our shared work and vision many years before. More recently, I have had the privilege of meeting the new generation of women politicians on a tour of the country, as part of a new initiative to interest women in political life, and it has all come full circle. It seems funny to think that we were trailblazers, but we certainly were, women. Women have so much to offer in political life and I like to think that we bring different skills to life in Dáil Éireann. I also like to think that the energy and commitment that female politicians today bring to political life is thanks to the efforts of women like yourselves, who do so much in the background.

So, thank you, Athlone Women's Group, for your steadfast support, for your commitment and for your willingness to forge a path for future women to walk along in political life. But thank you most of all for your friendship at a time of crisis.

Sincerely,

Maryor.

10. To David Henry,
gardener, Athlone

Dear David,

> 'Tis the ever green stately Magnolia,
> Its pearl-flowers pure as the Truth,
> Defiant of tempest and lightning,
> Its life a perpetual youth.
>
> — *Albert Pike*

I can't say I've ever heard of the poet Albert Pike, but I thought you might like this verse, because the magnolia tree that you have tended for so many years is now flourishing outside my kitchen window. What pleasure it gives me as I look at it and write to you. In fact, that is precisely why I am dedicating this letter to you, David, because you brought the tree back to life.

We both know that you have been coming to the house for many years now, for two hours per week to keep my small garden in shape, ever since you were a boy and you would come with your dad, when Enda was alive. Now, Enda is gone, but you are still going strong, the father of a new baby to boot. It's wonderful to see new life and I wish you many happy years ahead. Parenthood is the most wonderful journey, full of surprises, as you will discover. It isn't always easy, but it is rewarding.

The magnolia tree was a present from my friends in the Athlone Fianna Fáil Women's Group in 1992, a consolation prize following my demotion from Minister for Health to Minister for Labour Affairs. Looking back now, David, it wasn't the end of the world, but how I railed against it! The magnolia tree was duly planted, by Enda, and at first it seemed to flourish, but in 2001, Enda died, and the magnolia tree stopped blooming. It seemed to symbolise how I felt: that all the life had gone from me as well. I had lost my wonderful husband, my best friend, my adviser, my supporter. And every time I looked out of my kitchen window I saw, not a beautiful tree in bloom, but a stunted, withered object.

One day, you appeared as usual to do the garden and I said, 'What are we going to do about the tree?'

'Oh, I'll get that moving,' you said to me in your fine Westmeath accent and, not being an expert gardener myself, I let you at it. You got out your shears and you cut away at it, so vigorously that there was barely any tree left.

I saw a very sorry item when I looked out my kitchen window. 'Oh, David,' I said to you. 'It will never bloom again.'

'You just wait and see,' you insisted. Of course, I didn't know enough of gardener's lore to understand that the cutting back is to encourage new growth, but I took your advice and I waited. And I waited. And I waited! Two, three, four years went by and there was still no bloom on my magnolia. I began to doubt you, David, even as I saw you nursing the tree, feeding it and watering it and trying to coax it back to life.

I began to think that I really must do something about removing the tree; it seemed to me to be a part of my life that was now gone. Maybe the magnolia tree was sending me a message:

'Mary, I have fulfilled my role. Please release me from this earth,' somehow in the same way as Enda had been released from this earth.

But then, around the fourth year, you were in the garden and you said to me, 'It's going to bloom. I can see buds beginning to grow on it.' I was doubtful, David, but then spring came. One morning in April, I came into the kitchen, lifted the blind in the window and there was my magnolia tree, in full, magnificent bloom, with those wonderful petunia-pink and cream flowers. I have always thought that the colour of a magnolia flower is beautiful; that delicate pink shading to a deep fuchsia colour. It is a bit like life itself, I suppose, beginning delicately, having bright, illuminating moments and moments of dark shade.

Shakespeare wrote in 'Sonnet 98', 'When proud-pied April, dress'd in all his trim / Hath put a spirit of youth in every thing'. He was right – spring makes people and plants bloom. And on that April morning, it seemed to me that life had returned to the dormant earth, as life had gradually returned to me in the years since Enda died. So, I made a cup of tea and I sat out in the garden, marvelling at the colour and the joy that

that exuberant growth gave me. I recalled all of the years of my own 'flowering' in politics and in family life, and I came to understand what you had told me. That you have to cut back to the quick to enable growth to happen again. There was a clear message about gardening and about life: for both the tree and for me, expert nourishment and nurturing made us flourish again.

David, as you become a father yourself, I want to thank you for making the magnolia bloom again, and for bringing back memories of Enda, who planted it for me, of my friends, who gave it to me, and of the life that I loved. It seemed that the tree had once said to me, 'You've had your day, Mary, just go easy now.' But that was not to be. Life came back. I have the joy of six beautiful grandchildren; I have experienced the great pleasure of writing as well as encouraging a new generation of people interested in public service; I have taken on new challenges. Like the magnolia tree, my day is not done and my race is not run. Thank you, David, and many more years of gardening success to you.

Fondest wishes,

Mary R.

11. To Councillor Norma Moriarty,
Fianna Fáil candidate,
Portmagee, Co. Kerry

Dear Norma,

The 2016 general election is now over, and we have a Fine Gael minority government. Sadly, you did not get elected in your constituency of Kerry, but I wanted to write to you to thank you for your vigorous campaigning, and to encourage you not to give up. When we next have a general election – and who knows how soon that might be! – I hope to see your name on the list of candidates for Fianna Fáil.

The readers will know by this stage that I am not a fan of gender quotas, but that does not mean that I am not a fan of women in politics. In fact, the reason I met you, Norma, is because I was on a road trip to encourage women Fianna Fáil candidates and to offer my support. I was disappointed at the poor showing of women in the party in the previous general election, with not a single female TD, and I spoke to Micheál Martin about it, following conversations with Seán Dorgan, general secretary of the party, proposing my little odyssey around the country to encourage women to stand up and be counted.

In fact, I should add here that I am sorry that more women in general are not going into politics, from any party. As we both know, Norma, the number of women in Dáil Éireann at the 2011 election was a dismal 27. I am pleased that that has increased in 2016 to 35, even though our ranking in European countries is still only 17 out of 27, which isn't something to shout about. But we are making strides, Norma. Our numbers are growing at grassroots level and I feel sure that this will soon translate to the Dáil floor. Perhaps I will be proved wrong about gender quotas after all!

I like to think that our greater showing in this election is because women don't feel so discouraged by politics as they might once have done. When I was on my road trip, women told me that they found some of the gladiatorial behaviour in Dáil Éireann off-putting, and hopefully that will change with more women in the chamber. I also hope that more women TDs means that there are more men at home supporting them with family life; I know that this is what made my own political life possible; that Enda was at home and that he was willing to do so much. I feel very lucky in that respect.

But that's enough of the politicking, Norma. During my trip, I visited Mary Hoade in Salthill, Galway; Niamh Smyth in Cavan–Monaghan; Lisa Chambers in Castlebar, Co. Mayo; Jennifer Murnane O'Connor in Carlow; Mary Butler in Waterford; Fiona O'Loughlin in Kildare; Anne Rabbitte in East Galway; Claire Colleran-Molloy in Co. Clare; Mary Fitzpatrick in Dublin; and, of course, you in lovely Portmagee. Six Fianna Fáil women were elected on their first outing – Niamh Smyth, Lisa Chambers, Mary Butler, Fiona O'Loughlin, Anne Rabbitte and Margaret Murphy-O'Mahony – which is a great success for Fianna Fáil.

My visit to you stood out in so many ways, because I spent a couple of lovely holidays in South Kerry, near Valentia Island, and I will never forget them. My last holiday with my dear, darling Enda was in 2000, to The Moorings in Portmagee, and I can still remember it so vividly, because he died not long after. So, Portmagee has a special place in my heart and it was quite emotional to return there in September 2015, to talk to you and to John Brassil, also a Fianna Fáil candidate.

There was a lovely crowd at the community centre, cups of tea and coffee and lovely fresh home-made sandwiches – there was a great 'buzz' in the room. I was really struck by you, a young woman in her late 20s, so put together and determined. You reminded me of my young self in so many ways, as you are a teacher and a county councillor, just as I was when I was setting out in 1982, when there were very few women in politics, even county councillors, never mind TDs. I admired your dedication and your appreciation of the huge task you had undertaken, and of the challenges on the road ahead.

You had been selected by your convention and you were filled with such ambition and determination that you would do your very best to win a seat for your party, your constituency and your country. I know that you were not ultimately successful, but I hope that will not discourage you from trying again. Don't feel that you are a failure because you did not succeed on your first time out; learn from the campaign and use those lessons for your next attempt. Remember that you are going out there because you want to serve your constituents and your country. You are a public servant, Norma, in every sense of the word.

When I met you in September 2015, I know that I gave some common-sense advice about the campaign trail and about canvassing, which will hold true for the next campaign. Until that time, which may come sooner than you think, keep your spirits up, keep your health and keep a smile on your face.

1. Never wear 'bling'. Forget the dripping earrings and the flashy clothes. When you are campaigning, you are not going on a night out, you are talking to ordinary people on the doorstep, so good, work-appropriate clothes are best.

2. Always remember that you are engaged in a dignified democratic exercise, one that is as old as time. You are knocking on people's doors, and when they open, you have a message to give, which you need to give clearly. Tell the person who you are, what party you represent, check the register to make sure that you are speaking to the right voter, and ask for their vote. Treat it as if you were going for a job interview. You are the interviewee and the person who has opened the door to you is potentially going to take you on. Your voter is the boss in this exchange, but you are at a level of equality: you with your wares to sell and he or she with a listening ear. If the person asks for information that you don't have readily to hand, tell them that you will find out and come back to them – and do so.

3. If an argument arises, as it does so often on the doorstep, don't prolong it. Listen to the point of view being expressed, say 'thank you for listening' and move along. There is no joy for you or the householder in any exchange that could lead to anger. Anger is not how you would hope to be remembered.

4. Always think well of yourself. Not in an overbearing way, but believe that you are equal to the task at hand. Don't heap on yourself the woes of the country or the party; you are not personally to blame for any of them; if other members of your party engage in this sort of thing, rise above it. Politics has a way of throwing up strong friendships and fierce enmities; not in any deadly sense, of course, but in the heat of an election, it can seem that way! Pay no notice to any confrontations with rivals, just put a smile on your face and keep on going.

5. As a woman in particular, canvassing can be both trying and wonderful. You meet people you would never have met before; you hear glorious tales and sad ones and you have the opportunity to enter into other people's lives at a very intimate level. Use that wisely – do not squander it. And keep your sense of humour alive: many situations have a comical edge to them in the heat of battle, so enjoy them if you can.

6. Most importantly, Norma, your fellow candidates will usually be men, so, think about what unique skills you can bring as

a woman candidate. This doesn't mean that you have to be silly and girly, but you will be able to listen and to be compassionate to your constituents. And don't worry about any sexism you encounter; you will encounter some along the way, I'm sure of it; but that is part and parcel of life, as I can well recall. Meet it with dignity and don't 'engage' as they say nowadays. I know that it is hard with the world of Twitter, which I never had to face, but be strong.

7. Your family is the most important part of your campaign, your secret weapon. When you come home, wet, hungry and dispirited, I hope that you have a close family member to confide in and to tell them about everything that happened when you were canvassing that day. My Enda was that person for me; he was always there for me and in his mind, everyone else was wrong and I was right! That's not to say that he told me that I was just a great person all the time, but that he agreed with me when I just wanted to give out and let off steam. I hope that you found an Enda in your campaign, a shoulder to cry on when times get tough.

No doubt, you'll be needing that person again in the future.

Norma, it was a pleasure to meet you on that day in September last year and to meet all of the women candidates for Fianna Fáil. I know that not all of you crossed the finishing line in first place, or even second, but I am sure you gave it your all and that you were a credit to your party and to your constituency. Meeting you all reminded me of my own journey and, even if we have a long way to go, of how far we women have come and how much progress we have made.

> *Go n-éirí an bóthar leat,*
> Norma.

Maryor.

12. To my long-lost cousin,
Deirdre Lenihan Sloyan

Mary, Deirdre and her husband, James Sloyan

1

Dear Deirdre,

I write to you almost three years after we met for the very first time, at The Gathering, which I organised at the Hodson Bay Hotel for members of the Lenihan and Scanlan families. We have had many a long telephone call since, sharing our family history and connections and making up for all that lost time.

So many Irish families in the 19th and 20th centuries went to America to make a new life for themselves and often lost contact with those they'd left behind. I always felt that it was such a sad thing, the vastness of the Atlantic Ocean that separated people in those days, long before Skype and email, and the loneliness on each side. Colm Tóibín wrote so beautifully about the difficulties of emigration in *Brooklyn*, and I have often thought of that novel and Eilis's long journey to America and the terrible homesickness she endured, when I remember my father's brother, Willie (Liam), who left Ireland for America some time in the 1920s.

Willie was your father, Deirdre, as we both know, although until recently, I knew so little about you. When I think of all my visits to Boston and to other American cities over the years; if only I had known more about you, we could have met and shared our family stories. What a pity the wasted years were. Still, at least we are making up for it now, and that gives me enormous pleasure at this time in my life. I have never considered myself elderly, not even for a minute, but there is something about getting older that makes my family history precious to me.

However, as we both know, there's something of a mystery about Willie's early years in America, a full 10 years that none of us can account for. Who knows where Willie went and what exactly he did in that time? What we do know is that he lived in Chicago, where he married. His first wife passed away, and then he moved on to New York, where he became a journalist on the *New York Herald Tribune*. He was there for many years, making a name for himself as a journalist, and remarrying. You are the only child of that marriage, Deirdre. Willie's time at the newspaper was to be cut short when he fell foul of the McCarthy witch hunts of the 1950s. How extraordinary it is to know that he was accused of Communism in that way; Uncle Willie was very opinionated, like all of the Lenihans, but McCarthyism spread its net to every corner of American society and they were determined to root him out. How equally extraordinary to learn that that didn't put a halt to his gallop; instead, he made a new career for himself on the stage, starring in many plays, including a musical of *Juno and the Paycock*, and Arthur Miller's *All My Sons*. And on Broadway! Thank you for sending me all the photos of Willie on stage with Shirley Booth and Jack MacGowran.

Of course, you followed in his footsteps, appearing in so many popular television series in the 1970s. I had never realised that you were John-Boy's girlfriend, Daisy, in *The Waltons*.

Younger readers might not remember the show, but I used to watch this story about a poor American family avidly with my children when they were young and never knew that it was you, Deirdre. How I would have dined out on that in Athlone had I known! Now that I do, I think how like my sister Anne you are, and, indeed, how like my own dear father was Uncle Willie. Family resemblances are curious things. There you were living thousands of miles away in Los Angeles, looking the very image of my own sister.

When I was a child, Uncle Willie was often spoken about; what a great journalist he was and later a great actor, and I like to think that the two professions run deep in the Lenihan family. I wanted to be a journalist when I was young, Deirdre, and have returned to it lately; my father wrote many newspaper articles as a young man, and my brother Brian also wrote. Acting must also be in the blood: I always say that if you embrace the world of politics as Brian, Paddy and I all did, you are forever on stage anyway. Politics is a form of acting, in many ways.

You made a visit to the home place in Lickeen, Kilfenora, County Clare, and you write so beautifully about it in the little essay you sent me recently. It comes from the mid-'90s and it shows that you inherited Uncle Willie's way with words:

> Today is crackling with sun; I fill my lungs to absorb my father's atmosphere. I imagine him shouldering past other lads in the pub we now enter for lunch. In the grainy light, two men hunch at the bar like conspirators, smoke meanders from their lips ...

How beautifully you evoke the time and the place.

I couldn't really understand why Willie didn't tell you more about his family history, though. I wonder why that was. 'For a man fascinated by history, he had no history of his own,' you said. 'My mother, not a gullible woman, accepted that his entire clan had been wiped out by the Black and Tans.' I wonder why Uncle Willie forgot his family history in that way. I know that you have often spoken of the fanciful tales your dad would tell you about his family, which amused you later in life. Perhaps Willie had endured hardship during those early years in America, or was it simply that with his family thousands of miles away, they simply faded into the distance for him? That must often have been the case in those days, when it was so hard to stay in touch. I do remember that my brother Brian would often visit New York on business. Once, he was in town to give a speech to the UN, and Uncle Willie appeared, tape recorder in hand, to record his speech. Brian said that he was a brilliant conversationalist and that they'd chatted for hours.

Maybe it was simply that the past had no hold over him in the new country in which he had made his home. I think his family life in County Clare was probably unhappy. The children lost their mother very young and it is true that his and my father's father, P. J. Lenihan Senior, would have been a stern and unyielding man. They were all very well educated, but I wonder how much love there was in that house. I can still remember my father telling me a story about the death of his mother, Hannah. One day, my father and grandfather were coming home to Lickeen in the pony and trap, and as the house came into view, my grandfather pointed to the upper window. 'See the light in that window? Your mother's up in that room and she's dying.' It was true, Deirdre, but what a thing to tell an eight-year-old! And he added that when Hannah died, my father would be responsible for his siblings: Maura, Willie, Joseph and Gerard, who were like the steps of stairs. In fact, when Hannah died, Grandpa Lenihan got married again after a while, to Sarah, an assistant teacher at the school of which he was headmaster, in Gurteen. Now, Sarah was a formidable woman, and when she'd come to visit us in Athlone when we were children, she would frighten the life out of us. We all called her Aunt Sarah, because she wasn't really our grandma. She always singled me out and would pin me down with questions about school and whether I was progressing. Often, I had to read to her, while my siblings always scarpered.

We've spoken a lot about Willie's family on the shores of Lickeen Lake and that visit you made to the house and to the woman who lived there then, Mrs Carey. I was struck by your words: 'As we drive away, I look up to the upper window, hoping to catch the shadow of my father.' Like you, I have been back to the home place, to Lickeen, and have admired the fine two-storey house and thought of my father and his brothers and sister growing up there in the fields and the fresh air of County Clare. I think that the home place exerts a powerful pull, and, like you, I wonder how my own dear father was as a child growing up in that lovely place on the edge of the Burren, 'a great swath of Mars on the Irish Atlantic', as you put it.

I am delighted that we have been able to recall so many memories together, catching up on the lost years, and hoping that you will be visiting us so soon in Athlone, to share more memories of the fathers we both loved. Now that I have lost my sister, Anne, whom you resemble so strongly, I feel a great kinship with you.

With love, your first cousin,

Marjor.

13. To Ray MacSharry, former Fianna Fáil minister, Sligo

Dear Ray,

I am writing to you about an event early in my working life, when I was a 'rookie' minister and you stood up for me at a difficult time. You may not even recall this, but I have never forgotten it and I'm writing to you now to thank you. Everyone needs someone to stand up for them in life, particularly when they are young and green, and you were that person for me.

Way back in 1987, Charlie Haughey led Fianna Fáil into government and you were appointed Minister for Finance, with a very bleak financial picture in front of you. It is interesting that in 2016, with the bitter years of austerity and economic crisis in Europe now seemingly behind us, to remember that in 1987, we were in a parlous state, the so-called 'Sick Man of Europe'. Unemployment was higher than at the height of our latest difficulties, and we had massive public debt.

As you remember, the Fianna Fáil minority government had only just scraped in, due to the casting vote of independent TD the late Tony Gregory, and we knew full well that we were in for a torrid time financially. Much-dreaded spending cuts would have to be made, and I'm sure you recall your nickname at that time, 'Mac the Knife', which I believe you relished.

Now, as you know, the first meeting of cabinet is always held in Áras an Uachtaráin, and I can still clearly recall us gathered around the cabinet table, Charlie Haughey at the head. 'There is going to be blood on the carpet over the cutbacks we have to put into place,' he said, 'so if anybody feels squeamish, let them stand up and go now.' Needless to say, no one stirred!

I knew in my heart that my department, the Department of Education, as well as the

Department of Health, were to be targeted, as we were big spenders. Every single teacher and teacher pensioner is paid from the Department of Education budget, so the spend on staff is and was enormous. Difficult decisions would have to be made and I wasn't looking forward to them, especially as this was my first big job in government.

As you know, but the readers might not, when a series of cutbacks is proposed, they come from the Department of Finance in the form of proposals, and, to be frank, some of them are ridiculous. We all know they are and the way we tackle this is to argue and counter-argue over the cabinet table. And so, we come to '20/87', which refers to circular number 20, 1987, which I had to send out to every primary school in Ireland. That figure became engraved on my heart and my mind, and has never stirred since, because I knew that it was a mistake.

What 20/87 proposed was to increase the ratio of pupils to teachers by three in every primary school class. I knew that this would cause absolute mayhem, and I argued vociferously at cabinet to this effect, but I was told that no, it could be done; sure, what was an extra few pupils in a class etc.? Ray, as every parent knows, 'an extra few pupils' can mean less time and resources for their child, and less focus on the kind of learning that is so important for young children. It would also mean a reduction in the number of teachers, with larger class sizes. I knew that there would be trouble, and trouble there was.

The debate on whether to implement 20/87 started at 7.00 in Dáil Éireann in October of that year. Alan Dukes, leader of Fine Gael, stood up to say that the decision had to be rescinded, and he was followed, one by one, by his fellow Fine Gael and then Labour TDs. This was a blow, Ray, and a shock, because of the famous Tallaght Strategy. What this meant was that Alan Dukes had agreed with Charlie Haughey to support Fianna Fáil spending cuts, so that we could reduce the budget deficit. Dukes's words at the time were 'You don't play politics with the economy', and it is true that many have credited the economic recovery of the 1990s to the Tallaght Strategy. If opposition party members want to vent their disapproval, they can put forward a motion to defeat a government policy, such as '20/87', in private member's time; so they can make their feelings known, but it doesn't destabilise the government.

History, will of course, judge the merits of the Tallaght Strategy, but when it came to 20/87, did I feel that I had been 'shafted' to be the first minister to be castigated openly for a government policy? Well, it is all part of the cut and thrust, as they say, of political life, and I was fully prepared to defend my position, hard though it was.

Just as I was to stand to say my bit, at 8.00, I felt a presence behind me. It was Vincent Brady, then Chief Whip, who whispered in my right ear: 'Give in to Alan Dukes. Agree to their motion [to rescind 20/87]'. Within a minute, you came in, Ray, sat to my left and hissed into my ear, 'Stick with the decision we made at cabinet. Do not give in.' Well, there I was, piggy in the middle. I knew that Vincent Brady had been sent by Charlie, who was watching the debate on the TV in his office – the demand had come from on high, possibly because Charlie saw in this potentially defeated motion the beginning of the end for the fledgeling Fianna Fáil government. I was duly trounced in the vote and went home to nurse my sore feelings.

Perhaps this might sound like office politics to some readers, or that I am trying to settle scores, but that is not the point at all, Ray. I know that politics is full of twists and turns, deals and counter-deals. I was part of that world for almost forty years; the point is, that when I was under pressure, you backed me up. Everyone should have someone who does that for them at least once in their working life.

So, we come to the next day, and there was a Fianna Fáil parliamentary party meeting on the fifth floor of Leinster House. A motion was put down at the meeting condemning the dreadful 20/87, and, one by one, deputies stood up to condemn my actions in trying to push through this unconscionable motion – as if any sensible Minister for Education would want to increase the number of pupils in a class! Now, I knew instinctively, Ray, that I was being thrown to the wolves. If it suited Charlie, he would have let the criticism build up to a crescendo, and later he would have said to me, regretfully, 'We'll have to get somebody else into education, Mary, somebody who will stand up better to the rough and tumble.' Charlie would put the continuation of the government above the existence of any minister. I also knew that the average Fianna Fáil deputy knew nothing about the Tallaght Strategy.

To Ray MacSharry

The storm raged on and then you, Ray, got to your feet. 'Hold on now, folks, deputies and senators. I have something to say to all of you. First of all, Mary did not invent 20/87 herself. She was implementing a cabinet decision that had been agreed by every single minster around the table. The idea that she brought it in from a wilful act of her own is completely erroneous.' And then you went onto say, 'We are in the valley of death with regard to the economic future of the country. The Taoiseach here has made an arrangement with Alan Dukes that they can put forward private members for as long as they like and we will continue to uphold cabinet decisions. Isn't that so, Taoiseach?'

There you were, with your dark skin and hair, a nemesis to him. He nodded obediently. 'That is so, Minister. That is so.' There was a general murmur of agreement and we moved on to another topic. I was to live for another day.

Ray, I have never forgotten the way you saved me on that occasion. It wasn't because of any deep-seated love for me, Mary O'Rourke, but I think it was because you saw that your plan to bring fiscal probity back to Ireland was under threat if we went the primrose road of agreeing to Alan Dukes's Tallaght Strategy. Incidentally, Alan Dukes didn't want you to agree either – he wanted fiscal probity, of course, but also to allow his own members to express their parliamentary ire.

You told the truth, as a token of good faith, but you also knew that there was no one to stand up for me. I have never forgotten that, Ray.

How strange it seems to look back on those torrid times, even more so now that we have a similar situation in Dáil Éireann in the summer of 2016, with Enda Kenny and Fine Gael in a minority government, supported by some independents. What is it they say, Ray – *plus ça change, plus c'est la même chose*? The more it changes, the more it's the same thing. The wheel goes around, politics goes on and nothing seems to change.

In my own case, I learned a lot in those dark days of 1987. There I was, a rookie minister in the Dáil chamber, hearing those two competing voices in my ear, and I said to myself, which way will I go? My instinct told me to stick to the cabinet decision and I was right; but sometimes, when you are in a corner, there seems to be no way out. I needed to show my mettle and, thanks to you, I was able to do that. I learned that I needed to stand up for myself, even if I had to do it alone, but I also learned that everyone needs a champion, a person to take their side, as the saying goes, 'A strong person stands up for themselves; a stronger person stands up for others.'

As we both know, we could have gone on for a full Dáil term, were it not for Charlie calling a general election in 1989, encouraged by a few 'saucy' characters, as I like to call them, in cabinet, who whispered in his ear that we would sweep the country. He had a fit of pique, having been defeated yet again in a private members' health motion about giving more money to the AIDS crisis, and he was also emboldened by the success of a visit to Japan in spring of that year, when Ireland was proclaimed to be a wonderful country altogether. He was determined to return to power with a majority government.

Charlie went around the cabinet table and asked ministers, one by one, if they felt we would win. Along with me, you were in the group that did not want to go to the country, as I recall, but that no longer matters. In that election, we lost four seats. It was a gamble that didn't pay off.

Ray, 20/87 is indelibly printed on my mind, as is your support for me at that parliamentary party meeting. The lessons from that, for me personally and for the country, are as relevant today as ever they were in 1987.

With best wishes,

Maryor.

14. To Ronan Wilmot,
actor, Dublin

Dear Ronan,

I hope that you are well and happy in Dublin.
What a great night we had at the Gathering,
eating, drinking and talking. Is there anything
better in Irish life than doing all three, especially
around people you like and trust? I know that
we talked at length about my mother and
your mother's family, the Scanlans – it always
fascinates me how we love talking about family;
the older we get, the further we like to delve into
our roots.

This story concerns our uncle, Roger, but it begins with your mother, May, and my mother, Annie, growing up in Drumcliffe, County Sligo, at the end of the 19th century. Drumcliffe sits at the bottom of Ben Bulben and has been immortalised as the final resting place of W. B. Yeats, with that marvellous epitaph on his gravestone: 'Cast a cold eye on life, on death, horseman, pass by.'

Anne and May were to encounter early hardship when their father, Bernard, was fatally injured and stretchered home on a door from a pub in Sligo town; this was in the days before any kind of health system, so if you were injured or sick, home you went to recover or die.

Bernard had got involved in a row about Charles Stewart Parnell. This sounds so fanciful, now, in the 21st century, as Parnell died before the 19th century ended. My grandfather was secretary to the North Sligo branch of the United Irish League, a group that had sprung out of the struggle for tenant farmers' rights. Founded by William O'Brien, its motto was 'The Land for the People', and, as a Parnellite, my grandfather's passions clearly ran high. Bernard died as a result of his injuries and my grandmother was left a widow, with six young children and another on the way. This was before the social welfare reforms of Lloyd George, at least in Ireland, and there was no safety net for families like the Scanlans.

All they had was 12 rough acres at the foot of Ben Bulben, and I can imagine life would have been desperately hard. I have a lovely painting that hangs in the living-room at home in Athlone, of the clouds over Ben Bulben, which I spotted in the Oriel Gallery in Dublin one day. I paid quite a lot of money for it at the time, but every time I look at it, I think of my mother.

Thanks to a cousin who was a nun in the Ursuline Convent in Sligo, all five girls – May, Tatty, Chrissy, Annie and Bridie – received an education and, as you and I know, my mother and your mother May excelled academically. They were such clever women and I often wonder what they might have done if they had been born in a modern era.

Roger was the baby of the family and as you know, Ronan, the Scanlans were strongly Republican. All of them took the anti-Treaty side during the battles of the 1920s, and my uncle, then just 15 years old, was a runner for the Republican side. I can see him now, on the mountain, sent by his mother, our grandmother, to warn the Republicans hiding out in Glencar of any enemy approaches. Whenever there was an affray – and there were many – my grandmother would ready her dairy as a makeshift hospital. If the Republican soldier was dead, there he would be laid out; if he was alive, Grandma would send for a nurse or a doctor to dress any wounds. You would think, wouldn't you, that a widow with six children and no regular money coming in would have enough to be doing, but this story shows just how genuine was her Republican belief and what a tough, brave woman she was. The Scanlan house was known for decades as a 'safe house' for Republicans.

During this time, Brian MacNeill, one of Eoin MacNeill's sons, was on the side of the Republicans, while, of course, his father was on the other side, those that backed the Treaty. Brian and another five guerrillas were being hunted through the mountains of Glencar, the Treaty forces on their heels, Uncle Roger at the front, acting as a spy and guide for the men. Eventually, they were hunted down, a violent gun battle ensued and six young men lost their lives.

Roger led the men who carried the dead down to Grandma's dairy, where she laid them out that night. The next day, they were transported to Sligo Cathedral and buried in County Sligo. 'Sligo's Noble Six', they were called. Brian MacNeill was brought back by train to Dublin to be buried with his own family.

Roger then had to be hurried out of the country, smuggled on a boat to Liverpool and then to Australia, where he would live out his life working on the docks in Sydney.

In a twist to this story, Ronan, Seán Mac Eoin was the Adjutant-General stationed in Custume Barracks in Athlone. In a note, he ordered the Sligo Republicans to be hunted down, but that the 15-year-old 'boy soldier' should be left alone. I have never seen this note, but it is in Mac Eoin's own handwriting.

It is an irony that poor Roger had to leave the country, never fully to return, when his crime was fighting for a cause he and his family believed in, but the times were like that, Ronan, and the divisions ran deep. Some years ago, RTÉ made a documentary on Eoin Mac Neill – his grandson Michael McDowell, then head of the Progressive

Democrats, and myself were filmed in Grandma's field in County Sligo, talking about the effect of those long-ago events on our families. Michael spoke about what a tragedy it was for Eoin Mac Neill to lose his own son in that gun battle in Glencar, gunned down by soldiers in the name of the party which he, a father, now supported. Michael McDowell, with whom I had always got on very well, told me that his mother had spoken to him briefly about Brian's death, but that it was never spoken of in the family after that. It was a closed chapter in the sad, tumultuous life of Eoin Mac Neill. Isn't it amazing that all anyone remembers now is that Mac Neill gave the order calling off the Rising?

Uncle Roger's life was to be equally tumultuous, in that he never really found himself able to settle. When I was a grown woman with two young boys, Uncle Roger returned home to Ireland, nearly fifty years after he'd left. He was staying with my mother and he would come down to us for tea. It was summertime and Feargal and Aengus were amazed at the wonder of the short-sleeved shirts Uncle Roger wore!

Roger stayed with my mother for a while, then he wandered off to Sligo and then to your family,

of course, in Dublin, but he never found himself
a place to call home. He had been away for too
long and he had grown used to his other life in
Australia. I don't know if that could have been
called 'home' either, as he never married or had
family there, but of course, he had good friends
over the years, good workmates, and a life, which
he no longer had in Ireland. He just couldn't see a
place for himself here or a family of his own, and
so, after a few weeks, he returned to Australia.
I often think of him fondly, a small, stocky man
with broad shoulders, a great talker.

It is a sad story in many ways, Ronan, and readers
nowadays might not understand the passions
that divided Irish people almost a century ago,
or that political choices could cause life-long rifts
in Irish families, but they did. That is the reality
of the struggle for independence. But I would
like to end my letter to you on a humorous note,
after all of the 'heavy stuff' that has gone before.
When I was seven or eight years of age, I got
a notion that I wanted to stay with Grandma
Scanlan in Drumcliffe for a holiday. We had been
brought up in the town of Athlone and I thought
there was something mysterious and exciting
about the country, so I plagued my parents until
they relented and drove me down to Drumcliffe,

their admonitions ringing in my ears. 'Be polite, say "Yes please", and "No, thank you", and don't give any trouble.'

I was duly deposited and off my father drove back to Athlone. Bedtime came and my grandmother said, 'I'll go and get you your supper.'

I wondered what supper was, and was horrified when it arrived, a big, foaming mug of buttermilk, with thick curds floating on the top of it.

'No, thank you,' I said. 'I'm not hungry.'

'What do you mean, you're not hungry,' Grandma said. 'You are to drink that before you go to bed if you want to be safe and sound in your grandma's house.'

I tried feebly again, 'No thank you. I'm not hungry.'

She looked at me then with her gimlet eye. 'Drink that, or I'll bate you!'

Without another word, I drank every single drop of that buttermilk down, and off I went to bed. I have never been able to look at buttermilk since!

I am sure that Grandma Scanlan, having been through so much in her life, was not about to be bested by a fussy granddaughter. She was going to have her way and she did.

Slán go fóill, Ronan. We will meet again soon, I hope.

Your fond first cousin,

Maryor.

15. To Nuala Loftus (née Lally), childhood friend, Dublin

1

Dear Nuala,

I am writing to you on 1 June 2016, having just put down the phone to you in a rush of emotion. I can hardly believe that we have made contact again, after so many years. When I rang your daughter's office to see about getting in touch, her secretary very politely took my name and number, but I never imagined that we'd be speaking to each other just a few moments later. It felt like the intervening years just fell away and that we were best friends again, just as we had been for all of our childhoods.

Whatever happened to our youthful, growing-up friendship? I don't know how it ended and I feel sure that neither do you, but somehow our paths diverged. You went one way and I went another and I suppose in those days it wasn't as easy to keep in touch. Now we have mobile phones and we have email and all the rest of it, so it is much easier, but we never, ever should have ended the friendship.

Of course there was no formal ending, in case this sounds dramatic, Nuala. Instead, we just drifted slowly away from each other. I expect that in Ireland and everywhere there are lots of people who were close when they were young, who shared many life events, big and small, as you and I did, and yet somehow the friendship doesn't last. Life has a way of hurrying you on, pushing you to the next goal, crowding out your mind with so many things – children and births and sickness and illness and family matters – that you somehow lose the track of friendship, but I am determined once and for all to put that right.

You and I go back a long way, Nuala. There is no need for me to explain to *you*, of course, but for those who are reading this letter, I think it would be a good idea to describe the 'geography' of our friendship. We lived in Gentex, which my father managed, in the old Ranelagh Boys' Protestant Secondary School, which had been converted into our home. It stood in the yard of the factory, with its spinning, weaving, bleaching, dyeing and finishing sheds dotted all around it and its thousand employees coming in to work every day.

You lived practically opposite me in what was then the stationmaster's house in the old Athlone train station, now gone. Your father, Martin, was the stationmaster at the time. I can remember that the station was such a big, imposing grey building and it made us feel that Athlone was the centre of the world!

As I was growing up, you were my nearest go-to child to play with. I would go over to the Lallys' house or you would come over to me in the Gentex house and we would have our own childish games playing down among the turf stacks in the back of the factory, or sometimes being taken on the rowing boat with the grown-up children.

I was always fascinated by that house and I loved the mystery of it, with all the doors leading to mysterious rooms and corridors. There was a lovely big warm kitchen and small orchard and garden opening off it. I think there was also a sitting room, if I remember rightly, or a 'good' room. You climbed up the stairs and all the bedrooms were on the upper floor. So far so good. But the real mystery of the station house was that a big door opened from the bedroom landing right on to the railway platform. Each of your bedrooms looked out onto the platform and, at any one time, any of the seven Lally children could land out there to play. But not, of course, when your father was about, because he was of the old school of belief that children should be seen and not heard. They should know their place and their place was not to run riot on the platform of Athlone Railway Station!

Your father was the stern one, as we know, always authoritative, well turned out and courteous to his employees and to his passengers. Your mother, Delia, on the other hand, was such a lovely, soft woman. Whenever I would appear at the door, she would always welcome me: 'Come in, a ghrá, come in and sit down'. Now, I never, ever knocked at the proper hall door. I would knock at the kitchen door (my mother was very keen on her children knocking before they went into anyone's home or bedroom, so I would obediently knock) and your mother would usher me into the kitchen with its lovely smells of baking. I can still get that smell of scones or brown bread and I can still see them arranged on wire trays to cool in the kitchen. Your mother would be at one of her thrice-daily baking odysseys, because there was such a big Lally family. You would appear and we would instantly be giggling and laughing, sitting up at the kitchen table while your mother would be talking away to us as she bustled about, preparing dinner for seven children and two adults – nine people! That was a busy, busy kitchen.

You were the youngest in this family, Nuala, and you had three sisters and three brothers. There was Gertie, Joan and Breda, and the boys, Pat, Tom and Martin Junior, and then there was you. You were a bit like me, the tail-end of the family – a tag-on. Your mother had had six and then she had you; my mother had had three and then she had me, so I suppose that was a bond between us, that sense that we were the youngest in each family.

Paddy and Brian were friendly with Pat and Tom in your family, but nothing as close as you and I. We had our own young world when we were aged between six and 10 – those years in which we whispered our secrets to each other; those years in which we went into puberty together. Now, you were younger than me, I think, by about a year and a half, so I would have reached that stage before you, but I'm sure I told you all about it, and I know that we shared all those girlish secrets.

Then, when I was 12, my family went to live in the Hodson Bay Hotel. Oh, how I hated leaving you, by then my very best friend. Of course, the Hodson Bay was beautiful; on the banks of Lough Ree, the largest lake on the River Shannon, with its tennis courts and river views and all of the bustle and the comings and goings, but I never liked it as a home. It never really *was* my home. I expect it is always very difficult to make a home of a hotel, but my parents did the best they could and we got along.

At first, nothing changed in our friendship, Nuala. I still pedalled in every day to the station house on my bicycle, and your mother still greeted me warmly at the door, and life went on as usual, but then I was sent away to boarding school in Loreto Convent in Bray, the second big change in

my young life. I can vividly remember going over
to your house on the last day before I went away.
Isn't it amazing, Nuala, how childish memories
come back to us? I have never forgotten your
mother's face as she opened the kitchen door to
me, so lovely and open and always welcoming.
She never betrayed a thought, although I am
sure she often felt it, that here was the bother of
the Lenihan one again. But, anyway, I went in
and we whispered and we giggled and we swore
eternal forever friendship on this, my last full
day in Athlone.

I got up on my bike on that very early September
day and cycled back to Hodson Bay. The next
day I was wafted to Loreto Convent in Bray,
where I would spend the next five years. I have
always thought it incomprehensible how our
friendship ended, but looking back, I think that
my going to boarding school was the first step
in a very gradual parting, as life pulled us along
different paths.

I know that I have said this before, and I
remember writing to you about it many times: I
was always cold, lonely and hungry at boarding
school, but I had a powerful education, the very
best that could be given. I must have been ready

for it because I simply drank it in. The English, the Latin – I adored the wonderful Latin teacher, Mother Benedicta Corless. I can see her still in my mind. She was stern looking but she made Latin understandable and believable. I never forgot her words, that Latin was the most important language in the world and that all languages derived from it. I suppose in my early teenage years, when all girls had crushes on their teacher, I had a crush, improbable thought it might sound, on Mother Benedicta. I loved Latin and she, recognising a pupil who liked the subject, would give special care to me. I went on to do Latin for the Leaving Cert, getting an honour in the subject, which I also taught later on, but that's for another day.

I poured out my thoughts and feelings in my letters to you and you to me. We kept the postman busy between Bray and Athlone! You told me all that was going on in our home town; I told you how I hated school and longed to be back. Every holiday when I came back to Athlone, my first task was to get up on my bicycle and to cycle in the four miles to town to see you: all the way in to the wonderful you and for you, I hope, the wonderful me. We talked and talked, exchanging news and gossip, eating the warm, crusty scones and raspberry jam that your mother made.

Life went on. Your older sisters grew up and went to Dublin and joined the civil service, which was a great achievement at the time for girls, so quickly after the Leaving Cert. You were all so clever in the Lally family. I fell in love with Enda then, but we must have still been very, very close because I remember distinctly telling you one night about my love for him and you being round-eyed, listening to me. When my wedding day came along, which was to be 14 September 1960, there was never doubt in my mind but that you would be my bridesmaid.

Weddings were fairly sober occasions then. I don't mean sober in the amount of drink taken, far from it, but sober in the sense that there was none of the razzmatazz that goes with weddings nowadays. I look at pictures and brides have eight bridesmaids, all with flouncy frocks, and it is a thing to be wondered at. I had a good simple wedding. There was myself and Enda and Enda's best man, Eamon Doyle, his boyhood friend, and there was you, Nuala, my girlhood friend in your beautiful bronze-coloured bridesmaid's dress. The dresses were made by Molly Carney, who lived in Glasson, Athlone, and who is long deceased. Molly was a marvel: she had an eye for tailoring and for detail and our two dresses would stand the test of time if they were still about now, Nuala.

There we are in our wedding photographs, Enda and I beaming foolishly, flanked by you and Eamon. You had a certain bearing on that day, Nuala, which is evident in the photographs. You were very tall, but that never bothered you. You carried yourself well and gracefully, and, of course, you were a great giggler. I was a giggler, too, but I often kept it inside of me, if you know what I mean. You liked to laugh out loud, and we laughed at many a thing that day. We laughed at things the priest said (how awful!); we laughed at some of my elderly relatives, who had appeared for the day's festivities, dressed up to the nines. Needless to say, you and I never thought that we would one day be like those people, that we would one day be old.

We had a lovely, lovely day and then I went off on my honeymoon, and do you know, Nuala, I think that's what began to erode our friendship. I had gone on, if you like, to another stage of life. I know that at this time, you had joined Aer

Lingus, which was thought to be just about the most glamorous job at the time. You could not be an air hostess until you were 21, so you joined the ground staff, but by the time you were of age, you had given up ideas of flying. I guess that by then you had met Dermot Loftus. Your husband was a solicitor, a great big tall man, and he really mirrored your physique and your looks and was, if I can remember, such a good match for you. You had found the love of your life, as I had with Enda, and you wanted to stay put where you would see him often.

At this time, your father got a promotion within CIÉ, and the family were moved to Thurles. I remember distinctly going down on the train to meet with you and being disappointed that the magic of Athlone railway station and the stationmaster's house, where we had spent so many happy hours roaming the rooms and the platforms, had somehow gone. Your mother was there, still in great form, but somehow it was never the same. I suppose life is like that, Nuala. Things change and you can never recapture the magic of childhood days.

I was invited to your wedding and what a wonderful day it was. Somehow, on that day we seemed to regain our friendship. We swore everlasting fidelity to each other and we promised that we would overcome the gaps which had appeared in our lives. Yes, yes, yes, we said, we would always be the very best of friends. But slowly and inexorably, Nuala, our lives as friends seem not to have withered, that would be a wrong word, but to have faded. You see, our lives took divergent turns. I had family. You had family. You had your life in suburban Dublin and I started into politics and it became, as you know, all-embracing. I think that politics was to consume me for the next 40 years. I literally had time only for my family and politics. I have no regrets about that, Nuala, but how I wish we had been able to remain as close as we once had been.

I still kept in touch with you and would sometimes hear news of you from afar. I met your brother, Tom, twice, in Killarney, where he was Superintendent of the Garda Síochána. On one occasion I went to open a school there and there was unrest over an educational matter and he was in charge of keeping me in good, safe hands. We had a great chat, as I recall, and we marvelled at life in Ireland where you always come across someone you know from long ago. Tom had, in fact, kept in touch with Paddy, my now dear-departed brother, and from time to time he would visit Paddy in his bungalow on the way to Hodson Bay. Paddy always had great time for Tom Lally, as indeed all of us did for the Lally family.

I was so sad when your dear husband died. Indeed, many years later, as you know, Enda died as well, and you were so good to me then, but we lost touch once more. And now, we come to the really, really good part of the story and back to that gloriously sunny day in June 2016. I no longer had your phone number, but I knew that your daughter, Claire Loftus, had become the DPP, and so I called her office and there you were, as bright and cheerful as you always had been. I said to you, 'Why did we part?'

You told me, of course, that we didn't 'part'. There was no row, no falling out; there were none of the tears or the harsh words that sometimes girls will have for each other when they fight. We just drifted apart. But even in that five minutes on a crackling mobile phone line, we awakened such wonderful memories together. We talked about our weddings and our losses, of Dermot and of Enda, as well as of so many of your brothers and sisters and, sadly, of mine. Nuala, you filled in the gaps of all the missing years. We talked about our children, your five and my two, Feargal and Aengus, and I know that we'll talk again.

You said to me, 'Your voice sounds just like it did when you were Mary Lenihan,' and, to me, your voice sounded just as it did when you were Nuala Lally. How wonderful is that? And how I long to meet you, to catch up with everything and everyone, all the RIPs and all the births to be and all of that. I will find out how many grandchildren you have and what they are doing. You will find out how many I have and we will laugh about being grannies and talk about what it is like to be alone. Life will resume its rich, colourful pattern again and this time, at the centre of it, will be Nuala Loftus and Mary O'Rourke – friends eternally.

With fondest wishes,

Mary O'R.

16. To Robbie Henshaw,
rugby player

Dear Robbie,

As I write, Connacht rugby team have won
the Guinness Pro-12 and the province and the
country is alive with celebration. What a great
victory for the team.

You and I know each other very well, of course.
We share the same parish of Coosan, Athlone,
and, as you know, I taught your mother Audrey
in Summerhill College. Your achievements on
the rugby pitch for Connacht and Ireland have
made you a hero in Athlone, and a credit to the

community and to your school, Marist College. I know that you have taken the decision to move to Leinster at the end of the 2015–16 season, and, no doubt, further honours and triumphs await you, but nothing will equal the glory you brought to Connacht. Every young child in the province wants to wear the Connacht jersey, and the ultimate for them is to meet you after the match and to talk to you. You are a role model, Robbie, and you represent all that is good about rugby and about sport in general.

Of course, it wasn't always this way for Connacht rugby, as you know. I came across a piece in the *Daily Mail* in May 2016, celebrating the successes of the team, and there, in glowing colour, was a photograph from 2003. In this photograph are a number of people, young and old, including myself, all decked out in Connacht colours. We were all part of the Friends of Connacht, and we were making our way to the IRFU headquarters on Lansdowne Road to protest after the governing body decided to disband the senior rugby team. At that time, 2003, the team was considered to be a drain on finances for the 'cash-strapped IRFU', as the *Daily Mail* put it, but we were not going to go quietly. At the head of the march was yours truly, along with

Senator Terry Leyden, Senator Geraldine Feeney and Jim Higgins MEP, along with a host of other figures, including Eric Elwood, the rugby player, and pundit and PR guru Jim Glennon. I still remember the two young children at the head of the march, who would have been about the same age as you, and I can still remember Bobby Molloy's impassioned speech when we reached the IRFU headquarters.

I had never been in a march in my entire life, Robbie. I was marched on, certainly, and I was well used to protests about me and my policies, but to take part in a march, and as Leader of the Seanad, as I was then, was not something I thought I could do. But I donned my green scarf and carried my rugby ball and enjoyed every minute of it.

Enda was two years dead at that time and he would have been proud of me. You see, our connection with Connacht rugby goes back to the days when Enda was Honorary Secretary of Athlone Rugby Club, during the '60s and '70s. Much of our social life centred around the club, and I can still remember Enda sitting down at the kitchen table every week to write up the minutes of club meetings. It formed the background to our early married life and I have vivid memories of that time. I also regard myself very much as a Connacht person. I was brought up on the Connacht side of Athlone and I taught on the Connacht side of town at Summerhill. It is true that when I married a man from 'the far side', as we say in Connacht, I went to live on the Leinster side of town, but I feel truly Connacht born and bred and ready to rush to the cause of the province. When Ireland was finally settled by the English in 1653, the Irish were urged to go 'to hell or to Connacht', that land that Cromwell considered to be of little value. Connacht might be considered the 'poor relation', by some, but our spirit has prevailed.

I am pleased to say that the march received great coverage at the time and kick-started a strong campaign by Connacht people and a renewal in our self-confidence and self-belief. With our stay of execution granted, the province could regroup and begin to build up its clubs again, even though funding was an issue. Of course, one good club was Marist College, where you went to school – which played in the Connacht League – and that is where you played, Robbie, under Mick Loftus. The Connacht Academy was formed to encourage young rugby players, and your talent was spotted there. Everyone could see the promise in you, and when you were picked to play for Ireland, the whole of Athlone gloried in that. How remarkable it is that Connacht have overcome all the odds to get so far, and by sheer hard work and talent, under our brilliant coach, New Zealander Pat Lam. 'From Pro-12 cellar dwellers to Celtic king-pins', ran the headline in the *Irish Independent* on 10 June 2016!

But I am also writing to you, Robbie, to congratulate you on being an example to young people in Athlone and further afield. Much is said about the money in sport and the pressure to succeed; much is also said nowadays about how rugby in the modern era is such a hard, physical game. At the same time, youngsters look up to soccer players and GAA players and rugby players; they look to them to lead the way. Sportsmen and -women are heroes to young children. They don't want to hear that a player they revere has behaved badly either on the field or off. And this is where you come in, Robbie, because you are such a fine example to young people in your dedication to your sport and in the way you carry yourself; you bear the responsibility of your talent with ease and dignity.

So, good luck in this new phase of your career in Leinster, Robbie. Even though you have moved to the 'far side', as did I, to other side of the Shannon, you will always be a proud son of Athlone.

Best wishes,

Maryor.

17. To Mairead Blake,
my first cousin,
Tullamore, Co. Offaly

1

Dear Mairead,

Our uncle, Joseph Lenihan, was a double spy, a spy for Germany and then a spy for England. Now if that is not a startling opening to a letter, I don't know what is.

I thought that you, in particular, would like to see the story about Uncle Joe in print, because you love to hear all about our family history when we meet in the Court Hotel in Tullamore for one of our lunches. There's you, me and Gráinne, of course. We all get on so well and there's nothing we like better than gossiping and talking about the family.

We are fascinated by Uncle Joe, brother to my father, P. J., and to your mother, Maura. His story is an exciting and a tragic one, as you know, dying far away from his family in Ireland. I suppose some might use the term 'black sheep' to describe him, but I don't think that's right at all. Every family has characters in it. Every family likes to talk about an aunt or an uncle or a brother who was exceptional or eccentric. For the Lenihan family, Joe was that person.

Joe was one of five Lenihans, as I told my other cousin, Deirdre, in my letter to her. My father P. J., Maura, Willie, who went to America, Joe and Gerry. His mother had died of TB, leaving a young family behind. As the youngest, Gerry was sent to an aunt to be reared, which was not uncommon then. Joe was very clever, winning a scholarship to Galway University from St Flannan's in Ennis, to study medicine. He had brains to burn, but he gave up medicine after a year. Who knows why, Mairead? He was clever, but maybe he didn't have the appetite for all the learning that medicine requires. He didn't have the temperament, certainly, being given to tall tales of his adventures, and to getting into scrapes. From this beginning, the full tale of Joe unfolds.

Joe studied for the examination to be an officer in the Customs and Excise Department, passing it, of course, because of his intelligence, and getting a job there, which he kept until 1931, when he was dismissed because of a work scandal. Undaunted, Uncle Joe then sat the Employment Clerk's exam and he was placed second in Ireland. Of course, then his earlier dismissal was laid bare, so that was the end of that.

Joe then left Ireland and went to America to try his luck for a couple of years, before coming home to Ireland, where he was convicted in July 1933 for creating a public disturbance, and this was followed by a minor conviction for which he received a sentence of nine months in jail. Trouble just seemed to follow Joe wherever he went.

During the 1930s, the trail goes cold, but the next episode reads like a novel, Mairead. Uncle Joe appeared on Jersey, just before the German occupation of that island in July of 1940. He had worked as a labourer there, picking potatoes among other things, but when he attempted to escape from the island in a stolen boat, the motor flooded and he was washed ashore on the Cotentin Peninsula in Normandy. There, he was captured by German forces and interrogated. I'm not sure if he would have been able to tell them much, Maura, but we know that he was approached by two German officers who offered to release him from Gestapo custody if he would spy for Germany.

Perhaps the readers might be shocked by this and who knows why Joe agreed? Perhaps he felt that he had no choice, or maybe his wayward temperament came to the fore once more. In any case, off he went to Paris, where he was lodged until the end of 1940 near the headquarters of the Abwehr, or German intelligence, at 22 avenue de Versailles. Here, he received instructions in various aspects of spying and was given a cover address in Madrid, where he was to send any communications. According to Professor Eunan O'Halpin's book *Spying on Ireland*, Uncle Joe was to be parachuted into Ireland to give meteorological reports from Sligo, and then he was to do the same in Britain. He landed in Summerhill, County Meath, on 18 July 1941, and he went to visit his brother Gerard, telling him a cock-and-bull story about having been in Valparaíso in Chile, a story that he also told my father. Used and all as they were to Joe's tall tales, they didn't believe him.

When Professor O'Halpin's book came out, I came across this account of Joe's escapade in the *Irish Times:*

> German intelligence dropped Lenihan by parachute in July 1941. His mission was firstly to radio weather reports from Sligo, and then to travel to Britain to report on conditions.

> Instead he travelled to Northern Ireland and handed himself over to the British. Lenihan explained that, although a convinced republican, he disliked Nazism even more than he did Britain. His MI5 interrogators were amazed at his remarkable memory, describing him as by far their best source on German intelligence organisation in France and the Low Countries. One officer thought him too good to be true and suspected he was a German plant; others pointed to his 'moral courage', the honesty of his anti-British convictions, 'which he could easily have withheld', and to the quality of his information. (*Irish Times*, 2008)

I was a very young child at the time, but I do
have a memory, or a story that is part of family
folklore anyway, of Joe's return home to Ireland
when he was dropped into the country. The story
goes that during this period he came to stay
with my father in Athlone. The Garda had been
alerted about him and came to see my father one
night to tell him to get Joseph out of Athlone,
otherwise they would be calling to arrest him.
My father told Joe that he had to go and he took
my mother's bike, with the beautiful new basket
that she had just purchased for it, and he cycled
off to Geashill in County Offaly, where your
own mother, Maura, ran a two-teacher school
with her husband, Jimmy Blake, who was the
principal. I could only have been about six years
of age at the time, but what I remember of this
incident was my mother berating my father,
saying, 'I don't want to see that man here again',
or words to that effect. She constantly bemoaned
the fact that he had made his getaway on her
bike and that he had taken the beautiful new
basket that she had only just attached to the front
for her messages in town. Such stories stick in
little girls' minds and I have a vivid recollection
of all of that and of the excitement I felt about
Joe's escape.

We know that Joe arrived at Maura's in Geashill on the 'stolen' bike and that she kept him for a few days until she, in turn, was visited by the Garda, so he set off for Dundalk and the border. When he crossed into Northern Ireland, he turned himself into the RUC, asking to be taken to a representative of MI5. Here, the story takes yet another twist, as Joseph was sent to London and given the code name 'Basket' (I wonder if that was reference to my poor mother's bicycle basket!). He was put to work there sending coded letters to his Abwehr cover address in Madrid. Uncle Joe was now part of the famed MI5 operation Double Cross or XX, which was so important in winning the war. It would seem that every single German agent living in Britain was known about and contacted to spy for Britain. Of course, our relationship with Britain was strained at the time, due to our neutrality, and Professor O'Halpin's comments prove how difficult it must have been for Joe.

After a lot of toing and froing, B Division of MI5 finally decided that Lenihan/Basket was not a suitable candidate for Double Cross. Cecil Liddell, Head of MI5's Irish Section (B9) at the time, and brother to Guy Liddell, of course, was quite complementary about the Irish spy and wrote,

Though of rough appearance, he was fairly well educated, intelligent and with a phenomenal memory for facts and faces. He gave more fresh and accurate information about the Abwehr in The Netherlands and Paris than any other single agent.

I suppose that we can feel proud of that, Maura! Apparently, even though Uncle Joe spied for the British, he refused to take their money, which was typical of the man, but I cheered when I read what Professor O'Halpin said in the *Irish Independent* a few years ago: 'He was a wideboy but he had plenty of moral courage. There's no doubt the British thought he had a brilliant mind.'

His brush with MI5 didn't work out as planned, but Joseph was not interned for the war and was allowed relatively unsupervised freedom. We know that the British continued to give him fairly free rein in England, though he was under observation, and they even allowed him leave for a short holiday in Ireland, though there is no account that he ever took it.

When the war was over, the British settled many people who had been 'useful' during the war. They gave Joe a job sorting mail at a post office in Manchester. There he lived out his life, earning his salary, keeping out of trouble, but never making any communication with Ireland or with America where his brother Willie (Liam) lived. After all the years of fighting and trouble, Joe would seem to have settled down and made a kind of peace with himself.

The years passed and nothing further was heard about Uncle Joe until 1974, when my brother Paddy received a telephone call from the Garda in Dublin, who in turn had received a telephone call from the police in Manchester to say that a Joseph Lenihan had died in a boarding house there. Paddy contacted Maura, your mother, and you, and off the three of you went to Manchester, where Joe had lived for so many years.

At the boarding house, they met his lovely landlady, who had nothing but praise for Joseph Lenihan. She said that he worked hard, had very few friends and went to the library constantly. In fact, the library often telephoned the house with news of books he'd ordered for collection. It would seem that his mind had stayed lively to the last.

Paddy often recalled that Joseph's room in the lodgings in Manchester was sparsely furnished, but that it was a good, large and bright room. He died with very few personal effects, which I always thought was a sad thing, Maura. As we go through life, we accumulate so much: family photos, mementoes, gifts, but Joseph had none of these.

The Irish trio quickly made arrangements for Uncle Joe's body to be brought back to Ireland. Here I come into the story. Paddy and Maura and you had made arrangements for Joseph to be buried at Esker Graveyard in Lucan, County Dublin, and I can vividly remember going into the funeral home to see him with my two young sons, Feargal, who was 10 years old, and Aengus, who was six at the time. It was the first time they had ever seen anyone laid out, I think. I remember that Joe was tall, much taller than my father, with what I thought was a very refined face. There was a Mass in the church in Lucan and then he was buried in Esker. Professor Robert Dudley Edwards, then Professor of History at UCD, and father of Ruth Dudley Edwards, gave a great graveside oration – with his wild white hair, he looked as if he was born to give orations. Dudley Edwards's mother was a sister of Hannah McInerney, Joe's mother and my grandmother, so there was a great connection there. Dudley Edwards spoke very passionately about the Lenihan family at the graveside and we all felt a great sense of pride at this. Dudley Edwards had given Joe his place in the family, and that was fitting.

Mairead, as you and I know, this is not the full story of Uncle Joe's life, but just the bare outline, and many of the historical details come from Professor O'Halpin's work. It would seem that Uncle Joe's work as a double spy, a spy for Germany and then a spy for England, never really had any catastrophic effect on either country.

I'm not sure if this is a matter of pride or not, Mairead, but what matters to me isn't the spying, but the way Joe's life played out. What I think is so sad about this story – and I know you feel it too – is that during all those years he lived on his own in Manchester, the landlady reported that he didn't seem to have many friends. He didn't seem to drink a lot, he kept to himself, he read a lot and was a very quiet lodger. It is particularly poignant that during those years, my father made many trips to Manchester to the Royal Exchange, one of the international centres for the cotton trade. On many, many occasions he would have been physically close, I am sure, to where Joseph worked and later lived. I often wonder how my father might have felt, had he known his brother was so close?

And yet, Joseph never saw fit in all that period to contact my father or your mother, of whom he was very fond, because she had been a mother to him, as we both know. I wonder why he kept himself apart? I understand that you and Paddy found newspapers in his room with articles about Brian Lenihan Senior in them, which indicated that Joe was following my brother's career from afar. Perhaps he felt that he wouldn't measure up, if he returned? Or perhaps Joe felt that we would disapprove of his wartime activities. None of this is true, Mairead, as you know. We would have made so much of him if he had come home. My father, I know, would have welcomed him with open arms. My mother might never have forgiven him for taking her basket, but she would ultimately have made him welcome, too, and so would we all.

Whatever his reasons, I can only think of the lonely life he led. I know he seemed to be put together and self-contained with his books and his good lodgings and his small pension from the postal service, but he didn't have his family, and family is so important, as we both know – where would we all be without family?

Be that as it may, Mairead, that is the story of our Uncle Joe – his intelligence, his fancy imagination, which allowed him to invent stories about Valparaíso and having fought the Japanese among others. I often think he might have remembered that poem from school long ago, '*Tháinig Long ó Valparaíso*' by Pádraig de Brún, and used it in one of his more far-fetched stories. Perhaps this might explain more about Joe, that real life could never quite match up to that of his imagination; so much of him remains a mystery to us.

Now, as I write this letter to you, all this talk of secret money, radio equipment, a cipher, invisible ink and an address in Spain for communication purposes sounds so strange and so alien to us and yet this was the stuff of Joe's life, the background to that day when he landed in Summerhill, County Meath, by parachute. I am reminded of the lines from the poem by William Wordsworth, 'The Solitary Reaper': 'For old, unhappy, far-off things / And battles long ago'. Yes, when I write,

I am reminded of these long-ago battles and memories, not all of which are happy, but he was worthy of the memory we now pay him.

I never tire of talking about him when we meet, Mairead, and I know that we will go over those old, unhappy, far-off things again and Uncle Joe's story will be further enmeshed in our family story; it is part of the glue that binds us all together, which I think is very fitting. May Uncle Joe rest in peace.

God Bless, talk to you soon.

Your loving first cousin,

Maryor.

18. Eo Mo Mowlam, Secretary of State for Northern Ireland, 1997–99

Dear Mo,

I would like to open this letter to you with this quote from Maya Angelou: 'History, despite its wrenching pain, cannot be unlived, but if faced with courage, need not be lived again.' Those lines could be taken as a summing up of your own political life and the tenets by which you lived it.

I was fortunate enough to meet you on three or four occasions and I admired you so much: your life, your experiences, the way you met triumph and disaster and treated 'those two imposters just the same', as Rudyard Kipling put it. To the people of Ireland, you will forever be remembered for your role in the Good Friday Agreement of 1998, but to others, you will be remembered for your courage in dealing with your long illness, and for the way you engaged directly with people. You became a national treasure in your country and were loved by so many.

I know that you entered politics as a Labour MP in the 1987 general election representing the constituency of Redcar in Cleveland, and you stayed with it, and it with you, until you left politics in 2001. We first met when you came to see us as Opposition Spokesperson on Northern Ireland, when Fianna Fáil, under Bertie Ahern, was in opposition to the rainbow coalition government of John Bruton and Dick Spring. Bruton had been working with John Major on the first steps of a tentative peace process, following a great deal of hard work by John Hume, the man quite rightly credited with being the 'architect' of the Good Friday Agreement.

Your opposite number here was Ray Burke, then our spokesperson on Northern Ireland, and I was on the cabinet opposition front bench. You were the guest of the British Ambassador to Ireland at the time, and he had given a dinner party the night before to introduce you to people in Ireland. It was looking quite evident that Labour would form the next government, so of course there was a lot of interest in you, Mo, and in particular in your capacity as spokesperson for Northern Ireland.

We had all read and heard about you and we gathered on the fifth floor of Leinster House to greet you. You came into that room like a breath of fresh air. I can vividly remember you complaining loudly that you had to go and buy a pair of tights somewhere, because you had had a mishap that morning with the pair you were wearing and you had not brought a spare pair. You pulled up your skirt and showed us the errant leg with the long ladder in the nylon. There were giggles and red faces around the table and I had a quiet chuckle to myself at the brashness and the honesty of your approach.

Bertie's secretary was dispatched to purchase a replacement pair of tights and you went off in high good humour, but you also laid out the position, as you saw it, in Northern Ireland, and I was impressed with your grasp of the brief. I was immediately taken with your quick way of speaking and with your knowledgeable summing up of the key facts in Northern Ireland. In November 1995, US President Bill Clinton had made history by visiting Northern Ireland, and the ceasefire which had been in place for a number of months then looked as if it might hold. US Senator George Mitchell had come to Northern Ireland in 1995, of course. There were signs, Mo, of increased willingness to talk on all sides, but that fragile peace ended with the London Docklands bombing in February 1996.

For a time, it seemed that peace in Northern Ireland was a distant prospect, but a new IRA ceasefire in July 1997 offered us all fresh hope. Early summer elections in the UK that year saw Tony Blair and the Labour Party sweep to power. In Ireland, Bertie Ahern and the Fianna Fáil party were returned to government. You were appointed Secretary of State for Northern Ireland, and the rest is history. But what I hadn't realised, until I read a little bit more about you, Mo, is that you actually refused the position a number of times when you were offered it by Tony Blair in opposition: Northern Ireland was considered a difficult brief for any minister and perhaps you had hopes that your allegiance to Blair would be rewarded with a big economic brief. But fate was to have other ideas, and when you did accept your new role, you rolled up your sleeves and got on with it. To think that you did all of that, having been diagnosed with a brain tumour just months before the general election, is extraordinary.

Mo, you made such bold, extravagant gestures and we loved you for it. One of the first things you did when you were appointed Secretary of State for Northern Ireland was to fly immediately to Belfast and to a shopping centre in Royal Avenue. There, you walked out among the people; you spoke to them, you hugged the women and they hugged you back. There were tears and there was laughter. Everywhere you went, you made a big impact.

You set about meeting everyone who mattered, on the Unionist side, on the Nationalist side, on the independent side. You travelled south on several occasions to meet with Bertie Ahern and Minister for Foreign Affairs David Andrews, as well as Minister of State Liz O'Donnell, and you established very good relationships with them both. All in all, you caused quite a stir.

During this bedding-in period you came down to Dublin several times, and on two occasions you paid a visit to me at the Department of Public Enterprise. I was Deputy Leader of Fianna Fáil at that time, and whilst these were described as courtesy visits, we managed in a matter of a few minutes to have a real talk about life, about our husbands and families and being working women.

I noted the fact that you wore the wig that you had had made for you during treatment for your brain tumour with great insouciance, even though I believe that it often irritated you. In fact, one of the stories circulating at the time was that, at meetings, when matters got tense or perhaps incomprehensible, you would take your wig off and pop it on the table in exasperation. I liked that. I can only imagine what the civil servants or the other politicians made of it!

You and Bertie had a great rapport, so necessary in all of the talks in Northern Ireland, because they would be ongoing. They were to last for the best part of two years. You brought Sinn Féin to the negotiating table, and on 9 January 1998, you made that historic visit to the Maze Prison to meet with inmates of all political hues. It was a task beyond comprehension to some, because, until Christmas 1997, it seemed that such a thing was impossible. After the killing of Loyalist Billy Wright in December of that year, there had been a spate of killings, and the major parties could not even agree on an outline document of their differences. It seemed that all was lost. But, together with George Mitchell, who came up with a timetable of meetings between all of the parties, you broke the impasse that was developing among various groups, some of whom were prepared to go into talks, some of whom were not. You went in and talked in your straightforward way with them and the deadlock was broken.

I know that I applauded your actions on that day and so did so many others, but many of the media didn't like it. They thought it was showing off – grandstanding – and they thought it would not come to anything, but it did. Your intervention gave fresh movement and momentum in those talks and helped to move them forward to that day in April 1998.

We on the island of Ireland cannot forget that day when the Good Friday Agreement was signed, Friday, 10 April 1998. All of that is duly and heavily documented and it is enough for me to say, in writing, that we were proud of you, Mo, how you moved about among everyone and how you kept it all going. Later, you admitted that you felt that the men around the table – Tony Blair, Bertie Ahern, David Trimble, Gerry Adams *et al.* – assumed that the business of the talks was theirs to do and that you felt excluded. But I think that was because, after all, there were two prime ministers there and, at one stage, President Clinton, and you felt in a more subordinate role than you normally would be. There were many players in the whole Northern Ireland Peace Process and you were certainly essential to that. Your determination, your sense of destiny, your spontaneity in dealing with the differing parties and the – often potentially dangerous – alliances that you made; your plain speaking and your straightforward manner blew away much of the miasma overwhelming Northern Ireland.

The euphoria that greeted The Good Friday Agreement was enormous. 'Today I hope that the burden of history can at long last start to be lifted from our shoulders,' Tony Blair said at the time. Bertie Ahern spoke about 'drawing a line under the bloody past'. So much was said on that day and after, Mo, but it is the words of Bill Clinton, quoting from Seamus Heaney's play

The Cure at Troy to the good people of Derry in 1995, that resounded with me:

> History says, Don't hope
> On this side of the grave,
> But then, once in a lifetime
> The longed-for tidal wave
> Of justice can rise up
> And hope and history rhyme.

The overwhelming emotion in government here in the Republic was one of relief. After the years of negotiations and the many twists and turns on the road to peace, it had finally been brokered and we could look forward to a peaceful Northern Ireland with a parliament, and with proper democratic structures. In the Republic, we had a referendum to relinquish our territorial claim to the island of Ireland in our constitution, and it was passed overwhelmingly by the people.

George Mitchell, Bill and Hillary Clinton, Madeleine Albright, John Hume: we saw you photographed with all who had given so much to the process, but it is amazing how quickly the euphoria of that drained away, not from you, but from other political minds. I know that you received some criticism from some who argued that you stayed too long in Northern Ireland once peace had been agreed, carried away by your huge public popularity. Maybe that is true: many criticised your actions at Drumcree, in Armagh, when an Orange Order Parade was allowed to go ahead in July 1998; others felt that your visit to the Maze was inappropriate. Others still felt that your determination to bring Sinn Féin into the political process alienated the Unionists and that a softer touch was needed. Maybe Tony Blair never quite forgave the fact that you upstaged him at the Labour Party annual conference later that year when the whole auditorium gave you a standing ovation in the middle of his speech. I know the mentality of men in politics – that would have rankled, let there be no doubt about it, and I am sure it did.

Whatever the truth of the matter is, it became clear to you, Mo, that Labour, and particularly Tony Blair, no longer wanted you in the Northern Ireland job. Leaks began to emerge from No. 10 Downing Street to the effect that Mo's health was at stake and really it would be better if she left Northern Ireland!! Whatever the reasons, they seemed keen to get you out and to put Peter Mandelson in, who quite honestly didn't seem to fit the scene in Northern Ireland.

Now, when there is negative leaking, it is a very difficult thing to counter, and I know you found it extremely hard, despite having your family and your constituency with you all the time. Even though you said you wanted to stay for at least six months more in Northern Ireland, and possibly because you let that be known publicly, Tony Blair prevailed.

It would be fair to say, Mo, that you did not help your own agenda by refusing the position of Secretary of State for Health in 1999 because you had your eye on being Foreign Secretary. Many critics said that you were your 'own worst enemy' in some ways. Whatever the truth of the matter, you were shifted to a job as Minister for the Cabinet Office, a sort of a no-agenda job. Again, you had been hoping for bigger and better, but you went to the Cabinet Office with a determination to do well there as you had done in Northern Ireland and you did try to put a shape on things there, but it was 'a political cul-de-sac' as the *Daily Telegraph* described it.

You stuck it for a while and tried to do your best with one element of your brief, the drugs agenda, until a Drugs Czar was appointed and told by Tony Blair that effectively he was taking over that position. You also tried to bring the business of government into a more streamlined position, with government departments talking to government departments – until gradually you were told that you were meddling. Perhaps this was because, after Northern Ireland, you felt the need to 'do' something. The Cabinet Office must have seemed alien to you after the cut and thrust of Northern Ireland, and it must have been difficult for you now that your friendship with Tony Blair had cooled. I know that you had the strong feeling that he and his office were being run by the public relations department of the Labour Party, who wanted 'smart young things' in all the jobs and really had not much time for you. Perhaps that is true, or perhaps, as some pointed out in the many articles about you, the very qualities that so endeared you to the public – plain speaking, directness, brashness – made life in cabinet difficult. Maybe you simply rubbed your colleagues up the wrong way! And yet, there is a macho element in all parties that have not had many women members. I found it myself, Mo, in the 2016 general election in Ireland, when I visited and mentored female candidates for Fianna Fáil. One by one they all told me that they were both looked down upon and covertly bullied by some of their male counterparts *within their own party.*

I was very interested to read that you wrote a memorandum to yourself during your time in Northern Ireland, setting out the points that you wanted to pursue during your time there. One of your suggestions to yourself was to 'go with your instincts'. I think it's a very sensible approach and I know in my visits to election candidates around Ireland, I always urged them to stick with their instincts. 'They are the one part of you that usually won't let you down,' I told them. If you stick with your instincts, you usually come out right on the other side. How right you were about that, Mo.

Mo, you died in 2005, and I remain convinced that without you in the boiling pot that was Northern Ireland in those years from 1997 to your departure in 1999, the Good Friday Agreement would not have happened as equitably, and the structures would not have been put in place as thoroughly as they were. Of course, the work in Northern Ireland is ongoing, even 18 years later, but your role in beginning that process will never be forgotten. You will live forever in the minds and hearts of us 'down here' for your bravery, for your common touch, your breeziness, your bravado and, above all, your great big heart. These are all the attributes which made you the prime force you were, a gale sweeping through Northern Ireland.

We were only ships that pass in the night, Mo, but I was always glad to have met you, to have known you and to have observed the effect you had on tribal loyalties and on seemingly intractable issues. I am quite sure that your huge spirit and personality are out there in the ether somewhere, and that your lasting legacy is one of hope to so many people in difficult situations.

So long for now,

Marjor.

19. To Margaret Walsh,
political advisor,
Department of Education,
1987–92

1

Hello Margaret,

I can't imagine addressing you as 'Dear Margaret', so I'll settle for the more familiar 'hello'. It's a few months since we last met. You always so faithfully come down in early February for Enda's remembrance Mass and lunch in Athlone. I know that all of our friends and relatives love to see you coming, because you are a link to my Dublin political life. To me, you are a dear friend, but you are more than that: you were my supporter and saviour during my time at the Department of Education.

You came into my life when I was shadowing Gemma Hussey, who was minister in the 1983–87 Fine Gael administration. I knew a bit about education, having been a teacher, but of course I knew little about the passions and ideologies that lie at the heart of the system. What I needed was an adviser, someone who knew the system inside out, and who could give me the insight and support I needed. Lo and behold, you contacted me. At the time, you had been President of the ASTI, and were involved in the wider trade union movement through the ICTU, so you were at the coal-face, so to speak, and you got in touch to give me some unofficial advice about a forthcoming issue. I was impressed with your clear, perceptive views and by the fact that you were so definite – you possessed all the qualities of an advisor, Margaret, and I liked you immediately.

When Fianna Fáil formed a minority government in 1987, I became Minister for Education as you know. I can still remember my first day at work, when the official car arrived to whisk me off to Marlborough House, the former home of the Duke of Marlborough. What an imposing building it was; I was led up to my office by the Secretary General to the Department,

Declan Brennan, a fine, good-looking, cheerful man and an excellent administrator. The office was a beautiful big, lofty room, large enough to seat 40; I can imagine that the Duke of Marlborough had many a dinner party in that room! Into that office filed, one by one, the five assistant secretaries general to the department: responsible for primary schools, secondary schools, third-level institutions etc. Each had under his arm – his, because they were all men – an ominously thick file, outlining his responsibilities and what he had achieved, but more worryingly, a large section at the end which detailed immediate difficulties yet to be resolved. These difficulties seemed to be endless. My heart sank, Margaret, and I thought, how on earth am I going to learn all of this?

All this comes vividly back to mind, because, at the time of writing, Richard Bruton has been appointed Minister for Education, and I wish him well. I also fear for him, because unlike in his previous job as Minister for Jobs, Enterprise and Employment, with its clear-cut targets and measurable goals, he will find the miasma and the general waywardness of the Department of Education a surprise. I know, because I found this to be the case for me. Were it not for you, Margaret, I would have struggled to find a way through.

Readers might not know this, but the Department of Education is a curious beast. There are so many competing interest groups: the INTO, the ASTI, the TUI, the IFUT, school principals, boards of management, church bodies, parents' bodies, student groups. Each group must have its say and rightly so; education reaches into every home – every person has had experience of the education system and has a view on it. All of these views and interest groups must be knitted together, and, at all times, against the background of the prevailing economic situation. I have already written about how difficult the 1980s were – we were always striving for more and getting less – and my decisions would have been all the more difficult without your experience and your warm advice. It was a constant battle, Margaret, but an enjoyable and fruitful one.

The Department of Education is also a perplexing place in which to work, labyrinthine and, dare I say it, devious at times! The minister has to steer a careful path between the Secretary General, who runs the department on a day-to-day basis, and the civil servants who work under him or her.

To Margaret Walsh

You were an expert at this, Margaret, working through and with the civil service and yet watching out for me at the same time. Nowadays, a person like you might be called a 'handler', and sometimes in a derogatory fashion, but you were more, much more than a handler. You were also a sounding board. We would pore over the files that came up to me for signature and so often your acute mind would spot a difficulty that lay in the seemingly bland civil-service language. As minister, I would always read back through the files and be fascinated by the twists and turns that the issue had taken before being presented to me for my consideration, decision and signature. It seemed to me that often whilst the decision would ultimately be mine, in effect it was that of the civil servants.

In the various files, I began to pick out the comments of one or two APs (Assistant Principals) or EOs (Executive Officers), which I felt were particularly bright and acute. I took to asking the Secretary General if I might meet with some of them. 'What for?' was his response. 'Oh, I liked what they said on such-and-such a file,' I'd respond, and they'd be duly dispatched to see me. Now, you and I would often have a giggle about this, Margaret, because the civil servant would visit the Secretary General before coming in to me, and then visit him again afterwards. The power still lay 'at the top', and so it would remain.

Nevertheless, I found various ways to get around this, as you may remember. I took to hanging out of my office window and when I would see the AP or EO I was interested in, I would shout down, 'Could you come up and see me Tom [or Joan]?' They took to going in and out at different times to avoid me! As you know, there were so many truly excellent civil servants in the department; highly principled and motivated to do their best, for their department, their minister and their country; and while I had my own ideas on the same, and there might sometimes be clashes, you were always there to steer a path through this vortex.

We tackled so many things together, Margaret, including the NCCA (the National Council for Curriculum and Assessment), which had been set up as the CEB (Curriculum and Examinations Board) by my predecessor, Gemma Hussey. We restructured it and I took your advice to ensure that various members of the teachers' unions were well represented, to make the process of potential reform that much smoother. This resulted in much-needed reform of the Inter Cert as it was then, to become the modern-day Junior Cert. Of course, we fought our battles there, too, in setting up the body, which was a convoluted process, but we got there in the end. Ed Walsh was to be chairman of the NCCA and Albert O'Ceallaigh its chief executive.

Our greatest potential lay in the formulation of a Green Paper on Education, with essential reforms to the system. The Green Paper, as you know, but the readers might not, is a document that a minister sets out for discussion and debate, which, following a period of consultation, becomes a White Paper, with more definite proposals for changes in legislation. It might seem hard for readers to believe, but the only legislation in existence at the time was Stanley's Education Letter of 1831, written to the Duke of Leinster from the 'Irish Office' in London, which had its origins in legislation in the House of Commons.

> My Lord – His Majesty's Government having come to the determination of empowering the Lord Lieutenant to constitute a Board for the superintendence of a system of National

215

Education in Ireland, and Parliament having so far sanctioned the arrangement as to appropriate a sum of money in the present year as an experiment of the probable success of the proposed system, I am directed by his Excellency to acquaint your Grace, that it is his intention, with your consent, to constitute you the President of the new Board: and I have it further in command to lay before your Grace the motives of the Government in constituting this Board, the powers which it is intended to confer upon it, and the objects which it is expected that it will bear in view, and carry into effect.

As you can see, Margaret, hardly the language required for a modern education system! In effect, what Stanley's letter meant for Irish primary schools was that, if a window was broken in a primary school in Dingle, the manager of that school would ring the department to ask how that window should be repaired. That was the reach of the Department of Education! As you know, the idea came about from my regular contacts in the world of education journalism, notably the late Christina Murphy, who had complained about the lack of shape in education policy in Ireland. So, off we went, with our new Secretary

General, Noel Lindsay, who, along with his very able staff, began the process of drafting the Green Paper. As we both know, there were bumps in the road, Margaret, and I can still remember my disappointment at reading that first draft, and my rage at what I saw as the civil service waffle it contained. I mean no disrespect to the excellent members of the Department in Marlborough House, but you remember, I'm sure, that I ranted and raved about it.

John Coolahan, Professor of Education at Maynooth at the time, came to the rescue, putting some much needed clarity on the language of the Green Paper, but before you and I could take it any further, my time at the Department came to an end. Our Green Paper passed on through Noel Davern's hands, then Seamus Brennan's and, finally, to Niamh Breathnach, who oversaw the White Paper, *Charting our Education Future*, in 1995. Finally, a shape had been put on education in Ireland, and I like to think that you and I were at the heart of it and were in on it from the very beginning.

My abiding memory of my years at the Department was of the sheer amount of work that needed to be done; the huge, fat files full of facts and figures that needed to be pored over, the decisions that needed to be made, the sometimes stormy waters of a busy department that needed to be navigated. I could not have done any of it without you, my constant support. Any praise that I have received about my tenure at the Department should be shared with you, thanks to your warm presence and your wise guidance over those five years. There are too many incidents to recount where you were at my side, too many battles we fought together to fit in in this short letter, but it is the constancy of your support that I value most about this time.

I am glad that our friendship has survived those frenzied years and that we have sailed into calmer waters together. Thank you, Margaret. I am happy that you have remained part of my life and that I have remained part of yours.

Bye for now.

Love,

Marjor.

20. To my grandchildren, Jennifer, Luke, Sarah, Sam, James and Scott

With my two sons, Feargal and Aengus,
and their wives, Maeve and Lisa

Dear Jennifer, Luke, Sarah, Sam, James and Scott,

I am going to write to each of you individually in this letter, but before I do, I want to talk about the utter enjoyment and love that I have got from all six of you. It is very hard to put into words, but it is so powerful and joyful and free. I think of you always. I think of your triumphs on the playing field and in the classroom, which you come and tell me about with great pride and joy. I think of the great texture you have given to my life. It is no longer me, Mary O'Rourke, widow, and my two sons and their wives. It is me,

Mary O'Rourke, grandmother to six beautiful and wonderful grandchildren.

Now I know that grandmas and grandpas the world over feel that way about their grandchildren, so please excuse me if I go on and on about it, but for those who have yet to experience it and hopefully will do so, the door to so many delights will open up for you. Enjoy it. Revel in it. Talk to your grandchildren, talk about them, think of them often, because they lift many a dark moment. The clouds part and there they are with their bright grins and their shouts and their laughter, filling your life with fun and energy.

Back to you now, grandchildren. You don't call me Granny or Nana, but Mary, which is lovely. You properly decided some years ago that as everyone else calls me Mary, why should you not call me Mary? So there you have it. I am a grandmother, but I am still myself, and I like that.

Two of you live in Dublin, Jennifer and Sam. You live with your mam and dad, Feargal and Maeve O'Rourke in County Dublin. Luke, Sarah, James and Scott, you live with your mam and dad, Aengus and Lisa O'Rourke in Athlone. I meet the

Athlone grandchildren pretty regularly because Lisa is often in with one, two, three or all four of you, if I'm really lucky, or I go out to visit you all on a Sunday. It is more difficult with the Dublin grandchildren, because you are further away, but we have family get-togethers when I get to see you all. Of course, you are still my beloved and wonderful grandchildren even when I don't see you, because you are always in my mind.

Jennifer, you are the eldest, and this is something that you are immensely proud of. Whenever you come down to visit, and the six of you are all together, you will remind us all of this fact. And because you are the eldest, you deserve special recognition. You have a beautiful mane of honey-chestnut hair, and at the moment, you are tall, gangly, one would almost say, which is what happens to teenagers when growth outstrips their age, particularly girls. I try to reassure you that it will all even out in time. You are now in secondary school, which is a big leap for you, but I am pleased that you are in a Loreto Convent, because I know that you'll receive a powerful education there, just as I did more than sixty years ago. You know that I was never a fan at all of boarding schools so I am delighted that you are a day girl, with the love and attention of home showered upon you as you go about your daily schooling. As I often tell you, in the long-ago days when I was a boarder in Loreto in Bray, we frequently went by train to your school to play basketball and hockey, and we always admired the dramatic setting, with the views over the sea. Making the transition to secondary school can be difficult, Jennifer, but I know you are doing well as you tell me of various little triumphs along the way.

Luke, in Athlone, you are the eldest of your troop and the second-eldest by a few months to Jennifer. You are at school in Marist College and I am so happy about that, because it is the school where your great-uncle, Brian Lenihan (Senior) went, your Uncle Brian (Junior), your Uncle Feargal, your grandfather Enda and your dad, Aengus. All were products of that wonderful Marist institution, and you are following on in that great tradition. Now, I know you don't want to hear one bit of that, because you are simply happy to go to the same school as your friends, which is as it should be. You are very lucky; the school bus stops at the end of the road where you live and you hike up to it and off you go to Retreat Road. It is marvellous to see your independence growing.

To my grandchildren

We both know that the Marist has produced a lot of good sportspeople, particularly Robbie Henshaw, but you have chosen to go the road of the GAA and soccer and you have attained great honours in those sports. By the time you read this letter, your first year in secondary school and your first set of exams will be behind you. It seems to me you take your studies carefully. I don't really know if you do, but you give that impression. You are quiet and studious looking, but I guess that is only the exterior Luke we see. We don't see the interior Luke, which I think is fun-loving, bright and, I hope, confident.

Luke and Jennifer, you are both 13, soon to be 14. You are teenagers now and the world will change for you both in so many ways. You are no longer the obedient little boy and girl who heeded all that you were told at home, had your friends and went about school life quite happily. Now your heads are full of conflicting emotions that you may sometimes find hard to manage. Sometimes life at that particular age can be utterly perplexing. I remember that well myself!

You are lucky that both of you have dads and mams who have accompanied you along this road and into the world of puberty with its conflicts and overriding challenges. I know that they will continue to walk with you and to guide you along the way. You won't always want to listen to them, and sometimes you will rail against them, but you will still need them. Don't forget that.

I laughed when we were all together recently and both of you were telling me about your first school discos. Not that you were telling the tales willingly – indeed, they had to be dragged from you – but it seems that whether in Dublin or in Athlone, it is a real step into the unknown. What do you wear? What do you say? How long do you stay? All of the issues that you are now facing up to seem so important and yet, I suppose that in years to come, you will look back and laugh at how seriously you took it all. That is not to say that what you are facing is trivial in any way: it is all part of life and of growing up.

Jennifer, I can remember so well that your dad, Feargal, didn't really take to the discos and, in fact, having been to one or two, he quite firmly decided he didn't want any more of that, thank you. In your case, Luke, your dad was a great goer. Anything that was on that had life or music or people gathering, Aengus wanted to be there. We had endless people to the door calling for him: 'Is Aengus coming out?' 'Is he going to the disco?' And he went off always with a joyful heart and an anticipation of a great time. Two contrasting attitudes towards puberty, but thankfully both have worked out satisfactorily.

Now we come on to you, Sarah, Aengus and Lisa's daughter and one of two girls in my six grandchildren. You are just beautiful. You will allow me to be partisan, I know, but it's true, with your long dark hair, your wonderful laughing eyes and a great air of gaiety and joy about you. You are a star on the playing field; you play soccer and GAA and you run, you jump, you kick the ball with gusto – you love anything to do with the outdoors. I am so delighted that you like all of that, because you will need that spirit, that *joie de vivre*, as life goes on and gets more serious. Sarah, I have no doubt that you will break many a man's heart when you get older, but I have no doubt that you will enter into every encounter with joy and anticipation of what may lie ahead. I hope you keep that joyful spirit. It will stand you in such good stead.

Now we go back to Dublin and to you, Sam, Jennifer's brother. You are fair-haired, angelic, thoughtful, reflective and, for a young child, you show such steadiness. You are very loving towards your parents and to me, and you are always ready with a kiss. You are very studious, into your books and reading, very clever, and you take part in lots of school activities that involve the mind as well as the body. I like that about you, Sam, and I hope you keep that steadiness of purpose. It will no doubt serve you well in life.

You constantly amaze us with the things you come out with when we are together, which are so wise, way beyond your years and yet so timely. I think you are an observer of people and you wait your turn to say your bit, which is a very good trait. The world needs listeners, Sam, as well as talkers! You are also a great writer and whenever there is a letter of appreciation or of thanks to be sent, you will take your pen and colouring pencils and create the most wonderful card. Thank you, Sam, for that and for being you.

And now we come to James, the third child and second son of Aengus and Lisa. I have a little corner of my heart solely reserved for you. Why? I think it is because you came quickly on top of Luke and Sarah as the third child in the household and because of that and the huge amount of work your mam and dad had to do in the rearing of you all, I always wondered if you were going to be squeezed out or forgotten. But not you, James – you couldn't forget James! You love your sport, and you are really good at soccer, which makes me very proud, because, of course, your great-uncle Brian was a famous soccer player. Did you know that? He played soccer for Athlone Town and for his country, and was a great player. You, James, have the added advantage that your dad and mam bring you to every game and their Sundays are usually occupied with ferrying one or other of the four of you hither and thither for leagues and club games – wherever they are held, an O'Rourke child will be there. You are also a member of a lovely GAA Club in Kiltoom in South Roscommon, which is very famous for the training and care it gives the youngsters, so you have it on all sides. You are all my darlings, but James, you are my very *special darling.*

And so we come to Scott, the fourth and last (so Aengus and Lisa say) of the Athlone O'Rourke grandchildren. I am your godmother, a title which I asked Aengus and Lisa to give me, and your godfather is Lisa's dad, Johnny Dunwoody in Dublin, so you are blessed with two older people to act as your godparents. I always take the duty of godparent seriously, and this is my last chance to be a godparent, so I am keen to get it right. Years ago, I was made godmother to Pádraig Lenihan, my brother Paddy and sister-in-law Brid's eldest child, and I loved that role. In fact, I met Pádraig recently and he said to me, 'You were a very good godmother. You stayed with me with your Christmas and birthday presents until I was twenty-one, and you let me go then.' We had a good laugh about that. I had forgotten that I had been so punctilious in my duties, but there you are, Scott – you have another 16 years to look forward to!

Anyway, because you are the youngest, you are, to my mind, the smart one. You were talking earlier, you were walking earlier, you were shouting earlier, you were playing ball earlier than your siblings – all of the things that you copied from the three older ones. You were always a force to be reckoned with. I used to get such enjoyment from you in junior and senior infants when you would mimic your teachers. It was hilarious. Of course, I would always say to you, 'You can't do that in front of them or to them. You will get into a lot of trouble,' and you would fully understand that, but your eyes would be bright with mischief. Because you are the youngest and likely to remain so, you are a great pet in the family.

So, from Jennifer in Dublin to Scott in Athlone, what a range of ages, personalities, names and characters you have, a mix of youthful vigour, fun, thoughtfulness and enjoyment. I know full well that, as you go on in life, roses will not always be strewn on the ground in front of you: you will each have your challenges to face. You will enter into a phase of your lives in which you will want to be the same as any one of your peers and you will feel that to be different is to be wrong. Never, ever be afraid to be different. You don't always have to conform. Never be afraid to trust your own instincts, never be afraid of wanting to strike out and, if you possibly can, try always to do the right thing.

Remember that you all have wonderful parents, and, of course, other grandmas in Cork and Dublin, but that your Athlone grandma is thinking of you always, loves you to bits, and just wants the very best for you. Remember that I am always here for you, with a welcoming smile, open arms and a ready ear to listen to the latest triumph or ill which has befallen you. That's what grandmothers are for, to listen without any of the stress or anxiety that comes from being mam and dad. Remember that the road ahead might not always be even, but that you have within you the spirit and stamina for it. Remember to keep doing the things that you love and that make you happy, and remember, above all, to keep on finding the joy in life.

Jennifer, Luke, Sarah, Sam, James and Scott, I give you all a big collective hug.

Love,

Grandma in Athlone,

Marjor.